THE ONLY WAY TO WALK

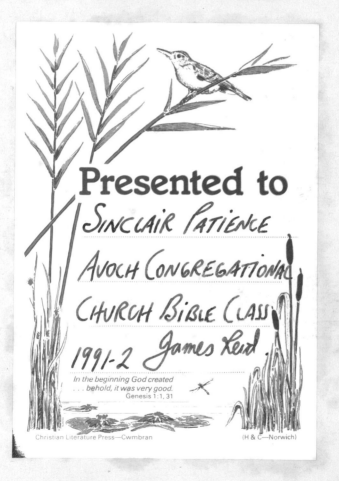

Presented to

Sinclair Patience

Avoch Congregational

Church Bible Class

1991-2 James Reid.

In the beginning God created
. . . behold, it was very good.
Genesis 1:1, 31

Christian Literature Press—Cwmbran

(H & C—Norwich)

THE ONLY WAY TO WALK

THE REMARKABLE STORY OF JAMES BROWN

by
SHEANA BROWN

CHRISTIAN FOCUS PUBLICATIONS

© 1991 Christian Focus Publications

ISBN 1 871 676 436

Published by
Christian Focus Publications Ltd
Geanies House, Fearn IV20 1TW
Ross-shire, Scotland, UK.

Cover Photograph
by
Ken Cowe, Peterhead

Cover design
by
Seoris McGillivray

Printed and bound in Great Britain
by Cox & Wyman Ltd, Reading

CONTENTS

PREFACE

A life on the high seas is hardly the background one would expect to find in the director of a factory in a small, insular Scottish town. Neither would one expect this successful business-man, familiar with the major ports and capital cities of the world to describe his beginnings as an apprentice barber, cutting hair and sweeping floors for a living.

Perhaps most unexpected, however, is finding this energetic and lively man, this eager sportsman and keen traveller, cruelly disabled; the victim of an appalling, crippling accident he has been the sufferer of continued pain and frustrating inconvenience ever since.

But the unexpected has continually imposed itself upon the life of James Brown, sometimes in more devastating ways than others. Coping with the effects of the unexpected has become incorporated into his lifestyle: alterations, both positive and negative never seem to come with warning or time for preparation.

How, then have these varied happenings changed him; how has he faced the "surprises" with which his life has been full? This happy-go-lucky traveller, this would-be hairdresser and returned emigre proclaims faith in almighty God. Having placed his life, without reservation in God's hands, he declares that he has found the only way to walk.

NOT MY WILL

Lord, make me willing to obey, no matter what the cost,
To follow blindly, if need be, although my case seems lost;
Oh that I may with steadfast faith grasp that dear hand of
      Thine,
And walk with Thee where Thou shalt choose - Thy will be
      done, not mine.

How easy when the skies are blue, and heart is light and gay
To sing with zest - and mean it too - "I'll trust Thee and obey!"
But when perplexing problems rise, and my heart is filled
      with fear,
Help me to upwards cast my eyes, and know that Thou art
      near.

Help me to see Thy way is best, whatever it may be,
For all that comes of good or ill is planned in love for me;
When fair ambition, heart's desire, lies humbled in the dust,
Give me the courage, gracious Lord, not to protest but trust.

For Thou dost see the end in view, and with unerring skill
Art working out Thy purposes according to Thy will;
Forbid that I with human thought should chart my own design
And choose what suits me best and say *my* will, *my* will, not
      Thine.

Lord, make me willing to do Thy will, and all my pleasure find
In doing that which pleaseth Thee with calm and ready mind;
Help me to act with motives pure, not seeking praise or fame,
Content to know that all I do can glorify Thy name!

Thus yielded, set apart to Thee, I shall be truly blessed;
My will with Thine in sweet accord will stand the fiercest test;
For when my course on earth is run and I Thy glory see,
Perfect and sanctified I'll say - Thy way was best for me.

E.S.Haddow, Ayr

1

THE ACCIDENT

"Right then, I'm off," James called to the lads across the plant-room.

"Enjoy the wedding," they shouted, trying to make themselves heard above the noise of the machinery. "Don't mind leaving us all working here!"

James Brown strode briskly out onto the jetty, the promontory on which the factory was built and headed for his car. He sank into its cushioned seat with a quick sigh. "What a morning!" he breathed. Without letting himself relax, however, he pushed the car into gear, accelerated away from the parking space and headed home.

It was barely noon on Saturday, 1st September, 1979. All morning fishing trawlers had been moored six deep in the berth next to the ice factory waiting to fill up with ice in preparation for their next week's fishing trip. At regular intervals the noise of the machinery had been drowned by the crashing of tonnes of ice down the exit chute into the gaping hold of a waiting trawler. One by one they had filled up and eased forward to let the next one in.

But the machinery had been playing up. Just at their busiest when the boats were taking as much ice as they could produce, a minor problem was periodically making the automatic system shut down. Every so often wet ice would cling to the sides of the collecting bin inside the factory and prevent more from being released. It only required a quick prod with a long pole to break up the forming ice but it meant that someone needed to keep an eye on it from time to time. James and his plant manager, Bruce, took turns to work at weekends and this was James' week.

"Just when I could've done with a quiet weekend," he joked. He and his wife Margaret had been invited to a family wedding and he was already behind schedule. Running a business certainly made some demands on the boss.

Having reset the machinery, James had finally got away leaving the rest of the staff to lock up. Then there was a quick change into wedding clothes, depositing the children with Granny and 'Dide', as local children called their Grandpas, and they were off.

The wedding was a large affair although most guests were from Peterhead itself or from the surrounding area. Living in such a closely knit community with interrelated families and extended church connections it was always hard for young couples to chose whom to invite and whom to leave out. James entered into the festivities and the family reunion that weddings so often become with all his usual vivacity. He and Margaret met up with lots of their friends who were Christians like themselves and they had a fine time.

About six o'clock James and Margaret slipped away. Another check on the factory would be necessary, just in case, and Fiona and Graham would be needing their beds.

Later that night at about 10pm James lay stretched out on

an armchair at home. It was good to get into casual clothes. It had been a long day.

"It would be fine just to drop off to sleep," he thought. "No. I'd better have one last look in at the plant."

As he rose from the chair Margaret looked up questioningly but with a good idea as to where he was heading.

"The factory?" she asked.

James simply nodded. He shrugged on his leather jacket. "We really need that production," he added, aware, however, that with Margaret no explanation was really necessary.

It was a still, calm night as he turned once again onto the jetty. The sound of the car door clapping shut made a brief echo in the harbour. It was deserted, only the hum of a boat's engine on the far side of the harbour breaking the empty quietness of the night.

The Peterhead Ice Company sits at the end of a short jetty which juts out into the middle of Port Henry Harbour. As he let himself into the building James knew from the silence of the machinery that it was again jammed. A quick jab with the pole and that would keep it going, at least until the next morning.

Using a high speed process which James and his father had imported from Sweden some years previously the factory produces its distinctive tube-shaped ice to sell to the fishermen of the north-east coast of Scotland. On the plant-room floor rows of huge steel cylinders grouped in fours reach high into the roof. At the base of each group of cylinders sits a large V-shaped collecting bin or 'hopper'. Each of the tall cylinders contains narrow tubes in which water is frozen. Then, flushed out by hot gas and the force of gravity the long tubes of ice fall. They collect in the hopper, having been chopped into chunks by a cutter which catches the descending tubes like a great bacon-slicer. The hopper, which is about fifteen feet long with steeply sloping sides, funnels the ice into its narrow base. Horizontally along this base a large worm-screw, about one foot in diameter powerfully propels the ice to one end. There it is forced upwards: a similar worm-screw, positioned vertically and encased in steel, slowly trundles the chopped ice up to the store. The whole system runs automatically, churning ice into the store without any need for manual assistance - unless, of course, something goes wrong.

James made his way past the big frosted pipes and valves filled with ammonia refrigerant. He had worked with it so long he could hardly smell the pungent chemical any more and they prided themselves that they kept the plant in good condition and completely leak-free. Ducking to slip past one of the steep metal ladders he could see the problem.

As before wet ice had formed on the sides of the huge bin until it had 'bridged' across the top, blocking the cutter and causing the system to stop. Reaching for the pole he had used earlier in the day, he stabbed at the ice and let it drop into the bin. He set the screw conveyor going on manual to empty it of ice and then stopped the machinery again. The cutter still needed to be freed. He hoisted himself onto the handy gearbox at the end of the hopper, leaned over its broad top and began to jab at the remaining ice. It was quite a stretch...

As he prodded vigorously at the ice around the cutter James felt something slip from the inside pocket of his jacket, hearing it land with a clatter against the screw blades of the hopper. It was his calculator, a good one he had got as a 'freebie' from some office salesman. Tut-tutting with irritation he put the pole aside and lowered himself into the bin, taking care how he stood on the knife-edges of the giant screw. He could easily turn his ankle if he slipped. There was nothing to be scared of, however. Quite often he had climbed onto the screw to get a better thrust at the cutter. Anyway, the system was switched off.

He reached down between the screw blades and fished out the calculator from the ice sludge. It looked undamaged so he stood upright again, placing his hands on the edge of the hopper which came up to about his chest. Like getting out of a swimming pool he'd have to lever himself out.

Suddenly, out of nowhere the worm-screw under his feet started to turn! It droned into action. His feet were slipping. There was no grip. His feet were being wrenched away - jammed between the sloping sides of the bin and the screw! Then with an unstoppable force his legs were torn from under him!

"They're being minced to pieces," his mind cried although no sound reached his lips. "I'm being dragged in!" Unable to resist, his whole body was being thrust to the other side of the bin and drawn downwards.

"Stop! Stop!" he tried to scream and lashed out with his

hand at the isolator switch across the hopper. He felt his finger touch something. Had he caught it? Just as he landed on his back on the horizontal screw the power cut out. The terrifying noise halted. The screw went dead. His legs, ripped off below the knees, followed his mangled feet, spiralling up the vertical screw at the end of the hopper until it jammed and the power died.

All was quiet.

For a few moments James lay in the silence, stunned by what had happened. As he heaved himself into a sitting position he looked down with horror at what remained of his legs.

Blood was everywhere - it was pumping out of his legs - and he could see his flesh coiled round the stationary screw. It looked so weird, so peculiar, he thought. Even now he was trapped - wrapped around it - firmly held to the steel machinery which had just drawn him into itself. He couldn't move. Then with a jolt he realised that he had no feeling. Blood...flesh...accident...there should be pain. But there was none! From the waist down he had no sensation although his mind told him that he should be in agony. Where was the excruciating pain?

Panic - mad, terrible panic seized him. Oozing blood was turning the ice left in the hopper to red sludge. As if to tell himself he was still alive he screamed and shouted.

"Help! Get me out!" he cried, thinking to himself all the time, "I must get out, I have to get out. Only Margaret knows I'm here. Someone must find me." Hardly knowing what he was doing he tore like a frightened animal at his right leg.

Ripping trousers and skin alike he clawed at his own flesh till he recognised his own bone bared before him!

"Hey, Brown, you're doing yourself damage here." Just as suddenly as this terror had gripped him he came to his senses. He stopped and froze. What was happening? A voice was speaking to him but there was no one to be seen: "You'll be all right. You're not going to die." James became aware of a presence, a nearness to him as he sat there, horrifically trapped. The voice continued, "You're still going to live. Don't panic...you'll be found...they'll get you out of here."

James knew he hadn't imagined this. Everything else was too frighteningly real! Not normally a mystical man he recognised the supernatural hand of God and was comforted. Such a peaceful calmness filled him crouched there in the hopper that seeing angels wouldn't have surprised him then!

Thinking clearly at last, he looked at the situation in front of him. His feet, his legs...trapped at best, lost at worst. Release was impossible. James thought of Paul and Silas, missionaries of the New Testament, who had lain in prison with their feet in the stocks. They had managed to sing praises to God. He cleared his throat:

Heavenly sunshine, heavenly sunshine
Flooding my soul with glory divine...

A new Gospel song he had recently learned also seemed appropriate:

THE ONLY WAY TO WALK

Because he lives I can face tomorrow.
Because he lives all fear is gone..."

("Who's going to find me at this time of night? It's
Saturday night. The place was deserted when I arrived.")

Because I know, I know he holds the future
And life is worth the living just because he lives."

Although frightened James continued to be protected
from the wild panic that had caught him earlier. He felt great
peace although he knew that he was getting weaker and
weaker. It was a strange feeling for one who had always
been so fit and healthy. Every so often he would stop singing
and shout for help. He checked his watch, trying not to look
at it too often and shouted every five or ten minutes.

Time dragged by. He was aware that he was losing a lot
of blood although no feeling had returned. He no longer
had the strength to keep up the singing. "Conserve your
strength," he told himself. "Keep shouting."

It was cold - so very cold. The steel of the bin and the
screw held the chill of the ice. He hugged his arms to his chest
trying to keep warm. "This is an ice-making plant, man," he
laughed at himself. "It'd hardly be tropical!"

Eleven o'clock came and went. James had been caught
in the hopper for almost half an hour. Into the silence the
phone suddenly sounded. It was linked to a klaxon inside
the plant-room so that it could be heard above the noise of
the machinery. Its hooting wail filled his ears after the
silence.

"That'll be Margaret wondering what's happened to me," he thought. The discordant blasts of sound filtered out of the factory again and again across the stillness of the harbour. Then it stopped. James prayed desperately: there was a terrible loneliness as this echo of the world outside broke off.

Time ticked by as James became weaker and weaker. Calling for help was becoming difficult. "They must find me soon!"

Down by the harbour two policemen were on their beat. Jimmy Gibb was a local bobby and with him was special constable, Alex Taylor. He had a shop in town but helped the police out at weekends. Together they had been checking over the quay and the deserted boats before they headed into town again.

Unlike many ports on a Saturday night Peterhead harbour was generally quiet as the fishermen set off home or into the town when the day's work was over. They would be back soon enough when the last hours of Sunday chimed away, ready to set out into the North Sea once again. The local bobbies didn't expect to meet many out at this time of night. After all, it was past eleven o'clock. Still they'd have a look over the empty boats and check out that klaxon at the ice factory. Just in case. They were nearly there anyway.

Across the bay on the far side of the harbour three engineers were getting ready to head into town having been working late on a boat. It had been a long day for them as they were getting the engines prepared for sailing in the first light of Monday morning. They were longing for a good clean and a bite to eat. As they had been packing up, however, they thought they had heard some shouts coming from across the water at one of the jetties. Could someone have fallen into the harbour? They were too far away to tell but they set off deciding to walk past the jetty on their way home. They had also heard the deafening klaxon earlier bellowing across the water. What was that? A burglar alarm? Could it have been coming from the same place? What was happening over there? They finally reached the Seagate and walked along in the dark between the streetlights. "We could just take a wee lookie in by," they agreed. "Just to see what's happening."

Just then the two policemen came into view under a streetlight.

"Hey! Have you heard the shouts?" the engineers called. Quickly they told the two policemen what they thought they had heard. They could see the factory ahead of them. A light was on. A car was parked outside.

PC Gibb took charge. "Stay here, Alex. I'm going in for a look. Something must be up."

Inside James clung to the promise he had been given that he would not die. He didn't feel too clear any more. The ice around him was so red with his blood that he wondered that there could have been so much inside him.

Suddenly, footsteps...a voice..."Anyone there?"

With the last of his energy James shouted, "Help!" "Over here," he screamed as the plant-room door burst open and he heard the footsteps hesitate. A moment later PC Gibb looked over the edge of the hopper at the gruesome sight. "Dearie me," was his phlegmatic response. "What's happened here?"

"Its too complicated to explain," James began ridiculously. "Get Bruce...my plant manager...here, take down this number..." He was gasping in the effort to get the vital words out.

From then on different people seemed to be coming and going. For a few minutes James was alone again as the policeman ran for help. Gibb grabbed the three engineers as he dashed out of the factory and sent them in, pausing only to prepare them for what they would see. "It's not a pretty sight, like. Just try and keep that man awake."

Even the few minutes alone for James dragged by. Was he found or not? Why couldn't he just sleep? He was feeling so tired.

Soon Jimmy Gibb was back. Bruce Forsyth wasn't answering the phone. What was his address? James managed to get it out but he could feel the policeman slapping his face.

"You're not going to sleep on me," he was shouting. The policeman looked down at the horrible sight. James' colour was awful. He looked like he could slip away at any moment. He must keep him conscious. "Hang on there. They'll be here in a minute."

Soon James was surrounded by people: policemen and doctors, ambulance men, the fire brigade. Bruce was there too, his face full of the panic James had felt so recently himself. Coming round a little James tried to tell him what was required. "Reverse the screw motor!" he snapped. "Change the wires. It'll go into reverse and you can unwind me."

James felt his nerve slipping from him as he looked at Bruce's sick and shocked face. He seemed in no state to carry out a delicate operation which might easily mangle his boss to death while he watched. The rest wondered just where they should start.

His own family doctor, Michael Taylor, joined James in the hopper as firemen worked round them. The other GP was there too and another was coming. Equipment was handed in and out of the confined space and instructions were shouted all round him. James croaked and snapped at them hardly aware of what all the activity was achieving.

"Come on, Bruce!" he yelled. "Get your finger out. I'm dying here."

One of the firemen hissed urgently to the doctor: "Hurry up and knock him out. We can't work with him shouting at us."

James was getting light-headed again even as the assorted drips pumped blood and saline back into his body. It was an hour since the accident had happened. He felt the doctor take some scissors to his leather jacket and rip it right up the sleeve.

"Hey. What're you doing there?" His voice sounded slurred. His head felt foggy and thick. As they struggled and tussled all around him James stopped hearing their shouts or understanding their actions. Could he relax now? Could he slip away into sleep? Peaceful at last and finally unaware of all the activity James slipped quietly into unconsciousness.

2

A CRITICAL CONDITION

Margaret sat staring at the white wall. Her pale face was devoid of expression but her eyes showed the tiredness she was feeling. Shafts of light were beginning to drift into the room through the half-opened blinds but she didn't look at them: they were too bright. She lifted her hand slowly to rub her eyelid. It was 6 am. She hadn't slept.

Beside her sat her father. Having sat at home with Margaret while James was taken to hospital, he had offered to take her the thirty or so miles to Aberdeen in his car as soon as his son-in-law was out of theatre. After several hours the phone call had finally come. James was out of the operating theatre. Could they come through?

They had just arrived. Margaret's Dad sat there now letting the night's events run through his mind again and again. It all seemed so incredible. James had come through to pick up the children only a few hours ago, his usual chirpy self, and now... He sat forward in his chair, his elbows on his knees, his hands together. Without looking at him Margaret knew that he was praying.

To Margaret the activity of the previous night now seemed like several days ago: the waiting for James to come home; her own frantic drive down to the factory, convinced that something was wrong; the serious faces of the policemen;

the crowds of people - firemen, doctors, friends - that had eventually come to give help; the painful hour-long wait while James' mangled body was extracted from the machinery; the fragments of the horrific story heard on the police radio as she sat in a squad car on the quay. Perhaps worst of all was not being allowed to see James or go with him and being sent home instead to wait for a call from the hospital.

When they had arrived the nursing sister had taken them into her office to speak to them. It all seemed to be bad news.

"He's lost a lot of blood...great shock...what we call traumatic amputation of the lower limbs...too early to say...prospects are not good, Mrs Brown. Prepare yourself for the worst."

The sister had then offered to go and check how James was and whether he would be able to see anyone. Margaret and her father sat together in the little room waiting for her to return.

The ward was beginning to come to life. Nurses scurried to and fro waking patients and starting the morning's routine. Activity. Yet she and Dad sat very still and quiet. Minding their own business. Praying that James would wake up.

"Mrs Brown?" The ward sister popped her head round the door. "Your husband has come round. Would you like to see him?"

Margaret was on her feet before the nurse had asked. Nodding briefly she walked silently out of the room and followed the nurse into the ward.

Screens blocked off the bed from view. Suddenly Margaret felt almost timid. What would she see? Cautiously she stepped forward. The nurse let the curtain close behind her.

Flat on his back, James was facing the ceiling. His eyes were closed and he was lying very still. Various tubes and wires were attached to his body. A monitor at the side of the bed flashed out its readings. She stepped a little closer to the narrow white bed, her eyes drawn irresistibly to the rectangular cage which kept the bedclothes off James' legs. What did it conceal? Then, before Margaret could say anything, her husband opened his eyes wide and cocked his head up. With a wide grin he greeted her, "Great to see you."

Amazed that he could talk at all, Margaret was soon hearing all the gory details of the previous night. He seemed to want to talk about it and tell her all that he could remember. Seeing that he was so bright and alert Margaret thought of her father outside.

"Dad's here too. Can he come in?"

"Sure," replied James before the nurse whom Margaret had asked could reply.

Eager to tell them about what had happened he was soon off again.

"I even remember waking up when I was down in theatre, like. I was looking up at some great big lights and the surgeon noticed that my eyes were open. He asked me if I knew where I was and I said, 'the hospital' and we had a wee conversation!"

"What? On the operating table?" It seemed a bit far-fetched. Margaret and her Dad looked at each other. Was this what they were to be prepared for?

"Aye. He asked me how I felt and then said he'd just put me back to sleep and that I'd be back in the ward in a bit." James grinned as he saw their horror and disbelief. (Nobody seemed to think that this could have happened until James met the same surgeon much later and his story was backed up.)

Tentatively Margaret asked, "And how *do* you feel, James?"

"Well," he replied," I didn't feel anything at all. It was really weird. I hadn't felt anything from the moment it happened."

"And now?"

"Now? Aye. Okay, I can feel now."

As if to change the subject James claimed that he could hardly see them and that he would get a crick in his neck trying to look at them while he was lying facing the ceiling. He called to one of the nurses to come and prop him up and with a quick fluff of some pillows he was soon sitting up and talking more freely than ever. It was only a few short hours since he had lost his legs.

As the day wore on more visitors, mostly relations called to see James. They had expected to see a dead or dying man but found James bright although he was still under some sedation. He enjoyed running the show from his bed and seeing so many folks but he began to flag and the ward sister furiously ordered everybody out.

"What are all these people doing here? This is an intensive care ward. Mr Brown's had far too many visitors for the first day. He needs peace."

When James was left alone he was able to piece together what he knew of the previous night. He had been told by the doctors what he already knew: that both of his lower limbs had been torn away by the crude tearing of the screw. After the firemen had cut him free the doctors in Peterhead had patched him up temporarily before rushing him to the ambulance. The job had been finished off and tidied up when he reached the infirmary at one o'clock in the morning. It had taken about a couple of hours for them to untangle and salvage what they could of his legs. Of his feet there had been no sign.

The surgeon said that they had managed to save his left knee and had amputated below the joint. His foot, ankle and calf were gone. But that was the good news. They had been unable to save his right knee and the amputation had been completed above it. It seemed that in those few moments of panic in the hopper when James had clawed at his legs he had damaged it beyond saving. He did not blame himself for it. He had been stopped from doing himself more damage and he was thankful.

Throughout the day he had recalled with excitement the strange and wonderful experience he had known after the accident: the certain knowledge of God's presence with him, the assurance that he would not die there in the ice hopper. Again and again he had told of the miracle.

Yet various miracles had taken place and even more was unexplained. Questions without answers danced round in James' mind.

How had he survived after the massive blood loss? He had been told that he had barely one pint of blood left in his body when he had been found. His heart had apparently stopped beating twice. Why wasn't he already dead? Why hadn't he suffered irreversible brain damage due to the loss of blood?

And why had he had such unbelievable freedom from pain as he lay unattended for an hour? Someone suggested that the small amount of ice left in the hopper may have numbed his nerve endings but this hardly seemed adequate. It may, however, have slowed down much of the bleeding.

He knew of no answers when he thought of how the accident had happened at all. Already experts had been brought in to examine the machinery. He was certain that it had all been switched off. And he certainly couldn't have started the power from inside the hopper. He wondered to himself how he had ever managed to reach the isolator switch when the screw had started up. It was barely within an arm's length. No more. Yet it hadn't been a collision by chance as he fell: it had been a deliberate, instantaneous act.

Most disturbing of all was the thought that the machinery could have started a moment earlier: that moment when his hand had been groping about between the blades of the worm-screw for his calculator. It preyed on his mind as the evening wore on. It was this thought that disturbed him as he fell asleep that night.

Affected perhaps by his medication or perhaps by the shock that had been inflicted on his body, James dreamt vividly and frighteningly that night, and for many nights to come. During these nightmares he often found himself back in the hopper. The machinery would grind into action as he reached down and he would see his hand being dragged into the screw. Headfirst he would be swallowed up as he struggled until he would wake up sweating and crying out. The nightmares would recur long after his physical wounds had healed.

The days following the accident were extremely difficult for James. Although his condition was no longer life threatening he was experiencing pain as he had never known it. His stumps were raw and dressings had to be frequently changed during the long healing process. He swallowed several painkillers whenever they were made available yet it was sometimes impossible to even think of anything other than the agony in his legs.

There was also pain that no painkillers could ever reach - phantom pains. They are something that many amputees suffer from as the severed nerve endings send confused messages to the brain signalling that the limb, though missing, is in pain. There was little that could be done for James. He just had to endure it and wait for the pains to recede. This, he was warned, could take a very long time. Meanwhile the nurses would find him stretched out on his bed begging for painkillers saying that his feet were killing him. The fact that they were no longer there seemed a mockery - a sick joke. Stabbing, crushing agony and all for nothing.

Although he continued to receive many visitors there was a real loneliness in this suffering. He could not explain sufficiently to anyone what the pain was like. It could not be shared - particularly the phantom pains. To James' practical mind they were irrational, obscure, even ridiculous. How could anyone understand when he couldn't explain it himself?

After a few days James was wheeled down to another ward. It was a general surgical ward with a number of patients in it. He even recognised some faces from Peterhead. Yet the familiar was mixed up with the shocking as he looked round the ward: car accident victims with horrible injuries lay next to unmoving, unconscious figures. James, who had never been in hospital in his life felt his stomach turn. He had always been repelled by injuries and disfigurements.

Quick to see the funny side, James looked down at his stumps. He was beginning to get used to calling them that. Somehow he hadn't felt squeamish about them at all. He supposed his legs had looked so gruesome while he sat in the hopper that anything was an improvement.

Between visitors, or dressing changes, or meals, or when he was unable to sleep James would often daydream. It helped to take his mind away from the pain and gave a bit of freedom which being tied to his bed denied him. Perhaps being so close to death encouraged him to be nostalgic. "Anyway," he thought, "plenty time to think now."

3
CHOICES

Unlike the majority of folk from Peterhead James had not been born in the area. His father, Robert Brown, was a native of Musselburgh who only moved his young family north to his wife's home town when James was about a year old. Although he was a hairdresser to trade Robert soon joined his in-laws at the fishing. He'd always had a liking for boats and he quickly mastered the new job and life at sea.

It meant, however, that he was often away from home for most of the week. Weekends were usually the only times that these men saw their families. In houses where working sons joined their fathers and uncles on the boats the week could pass very quietly until they came home. Perhaps for this reason there was always a strong community spirit in the fishing villages of the east coast. Wives and mothers met up frequently midweek; grandparents joined in the rearing of young children; the men at sea lived in each other's pockets for days on end.

Mixed with all this was the intense religiosity of the area. When Robert Brown moved to Peterhead he and his wife found an array of evangelical churches and 'meetings' from which to chose, for they were both Christians and wanted to find a suitable place to worship. Brethren groups of varying degrees of strictness in their codes of practice existed side by side; the more traditional parish churches, the 'Muckle Kirk', housed substantial memberships in the same streets; Baptists and Congregationalists were scattered liberally throughout. It was said of Peterhead (and it may still be true) that it had more churches than pubs - an unusual occurrence in any area.

Primarily, however, Peterhead was a Brethren stronghold. Through various revivals spreading along the east coast of Scotland, many assemblies had been set up. Because of their large memberships the activity of the town was often shaped by shades of Brethren opinion: town councillors would be unwise to suggest community programmes which might contradict their beliefs; school teachers who initiated a trip to see an educational film or a school dance would be hastily discouraged; observance of the Lord's Day with respect to work was of great importance. In general this latter view was strictly upheld by the whole evangelical majority and it often had far-reaching results, particularly with regard to the fishing.

Fishing was the largest single employer in Peterhead and in many other coastal towns. Many families owed their entire livelihood to the sea. Nevertheless, few vessels would sail from port to begin the week's work until midnight had been passed on Sunday night. Then as the first hours of Monday morning dawned, they would sail out of harbour. Bright lights would illuminate the boats against the night sky. Sweethearts and mothers sometimes huddled down at the quay, inky shapes in the darkness, to wave goodbye. Even in bad weather or enduring poor harvests of fish Sunday fishing was anathema to them. It remained the practice of only a small, censured minority.

The Browns had been involved in different churches prior to their marriage: Robert in the Assemblies of God, and Jeanie, his wife, in the Church of Christ. It was the Pentecostal Assembly of God church that they chose to join when they travelled north. The nearest Assembly was at Cairnbulg, seventeen miles away so they travelled there each week to worship.

There were only a few Pentecostal churches in the area at that time. An ex-missionary named Alan Benson started the Assemblies in the North-East and after the war an Assembly of God church began in Peterhead itself. James' parents were very involved in its beginnings. In their home not long after they arrived in Peterhead a group began to meet and in the early fifties an Assembly of God campaign was held in Peterhead. Visiting speakers stayed with the Browns and James and his brother often sat listening to them as they chatted with their father and his friends in the house. It was less fun sitting through the sermons - but hearing them talk in the house was fine!

At one stage Alan Benson came to stay with James' parents for six months. He had been a missionary in China and he told stories of his time there which fascinated James: stories of travelling there by sea; of cities which were even then crowded with people; of travelling for days and weeks into remote villages where people had never heard of Jesus. There were also stories which he seldom told of imprisonment and brutal torture which he had recently endured under the Japanese invaders of China for being a missionary. His main reason for coming to Peterhead at this time was to recuperate after this dreadful ordeal.

As the Assembly of God church grew they began to meet in a hall in Peterhead, the Ebenezer Hall. Alan Benson often spoke there during his stay with the Browns and in some areas members of the new church became known as the 'Bensonites' after this man. They were also nick-named 'Penties' or 'Ebenezer's' for meeting in the hall in Peterhead. The nick-names were generally all in good fun yet there was a certain amount of opposition to the new Assembly of God church.

This was partly because of the new practices they introduced and partly because they did not restrict the Sacrament of the Lord's Supper to their own members. Instead they had what was known as an 'open table'. This was a contentious issue amongst some of the local churches where communion was only offered to those of their own membership or who submitted proof of their membership in a similar church or meeting. This new church which was breaking with this practice was unpopular. Even at school James was teased with these religious nick-names. But he did not mind. The intricacies of Christian practices did not bother him. He had heard for the first time of far away lands and of travelling across the sea. Not that he wanted to be a missionary. He had decided that whatever happened, he wanted to see the world.

It was certainly a strict environment in which to bring up children and the lifestyle was sheltered. Yet to James and his brother, Robert and their friends it was just what they were used to. Going to church and keeping Sunday special were second nature to them; learning Bible verses was something they all did with even poetry lessons at school consisting of learning hymns and Bible texts; keeping away from things of which their parents and grandparents disapproved was no great hardship when they preferred to be walking the dogs or splashing about in the sea anyway.

At the age of eleven James was baptised having professed faith in Jesus Christ. Although he was young he wanted to make this commitment. It seemed so natural. As children Christ's parable of the narrow and broad paths had always been made very clear: he was either on the road to heaven or the road to hell. Choosing heaven was so simple.

Other choices, less simple were to be made or were being made for him by the time he left school. James still had that early longing to go to sea and travel the world. If anything the dreams had grown and been bolstered during Geography lessons at school and by listening to older friends home from the Navy, full of stories and loaded with the pay they could not spend at sea. His parents, however, were keen for him to stay at home so for a while he went onto the boats, working with his uncle on a herring drifter. The youngest lad was always called the 'coiler' and he was given the heavy, wet ropes to wind up. It was a long, laborious job. And James had one serious problem - he was seasick! In the cramped, smelly conditions of the fishing boats he felt permanently ill. The older fishermen would tease him: "You want to tak' a coo by the tail and git awa' tae the coontry!"

They were right. James had to leave the fishing - and fast!

His father had always been keen to start his own hairdressing business since coming to Peterhead. The next suggestion put to James was that he and his father should go into partnership together and buy a barber's shop. The idea did not suit James at all. A barber? By this time all he wanted was to be an engineer, his hands thick with grease and engine oil. Was it to be Brylcreem and hair oil instead? As no apprenticeships were forthcoming in engineering, James finally agreed to his father's plan. Although his Dad could not force him any longer, fondness for his mother made him give in. For as long as he could remember she had been unwell, first undergoing a massive stomach operation and thereafter prone to weakness and fainting fits on a regular basis. He had ceased to be alarmed by them - it was something they all just accepted. But James was a shy boy and also one who disliked causing an unnecessary rumpus. If his mother wanted her elder son with her for as long as possible then he said he would give it a try. There was always plenty time.

First of all he would need to learn his trade. He was given an apprenticeship with the biggest hairdressing shop in Peterhead, Andrew Cordiner's. He was a friend of James' father and he agreed to train him. James would also have to spend three nights a week at night classes at a college in Aberdeen. And so his training began.

How shy he was at those night classes. There were so many girls! The few boys stuck together and coyly avoided them. Even going through in the bus from Peterhead they rarely spoke. James got into conversation with some of them now and again but it was usually embarrassing.

"Are you doing ladies an' all?" they would giggle.

"Aye, aye."

"Do you practice doing home perms on your Mum then?"

James would retire helplessly into a desperate silence. The same painful process happened week after week.

James always dreaded Saturdays at work. Home from a week's fishing the male community seemed to congregate *en mass* for a haircut or a shave. Queues would spill out of the door onto the street and it would become quite a social event. Inside, however, for the harassed apprentice it was hectic as James' lack of confidence became more pronounced in the rush. He was never allowed to do much - just a go now and again on some of the old men who weren't too fussy anyway. Sweeping the floor of all the clipped curls and hair, poking his brush under stools and round the feet of those waiting, James protested inwardly that this was 'too sissy' a job. He wanted out.

After four months he had to tell his father and his boss that hairdressing was not for him. What a relief! At the right time an interview with a local food factory came up for a new apprenticeship, as an engineer. He was given the job and again attended night school - with not a girl in sight!

Living on the coast and surrounded by boats of all sorts, he could not get his longing for the sea out of his system. More friends appeared home on leave from the Merchant Navy. Sometimes they would take James with them when they went out. They would talk of sunny, exotic lands where they did what they pleased. Free from the restrictions of home they seemed to live as they chose and spent their hoarded cash when they returned. They always had plenty money to splash around. More and more James was hankering to get away from home. The whole town, where everyone knew everything about him seemed so claustrophobic in comparison, so dull. Church too did not hold his interest any more although he didn't dare do the things that the others did. He just kept it all inside and wished he wasn't there.

The engineering training lasted for five years and he specialised in electrical engineering. Surrounded by yards of cable and wire and multicoloured flex he was in his element. Yet again his plans were to be changed.

Called out of the plant-room one day by his boss, James was asked to take a small test.

"Nothing to worry about, Jim. Just look at these pictures and tell me what you see."

It was a book of colour drawings, each page showing bubbles of colour shaped into a circle.

"Seven," he replied, as the number seemed to jump out of the jumbled colours. "Five" and again "Two" as he turned the pages of the book.

James could tell that his answers were for some reason not what his boss wanted to hear. Why? What was wrong? He was told, and it was soon confirmed, that he, a trainee electrical engineer, whose job relied upon correctly and safely wiring equipment, who depended upon knowing one strand of wire from another, was colour blind. In few jobs would this matter but in this one it was crucial. Though he had not yet made a mistake he knew that he would never be confident in his work.

It would mean another change. Thankfully, though he preferred the choice he had made, he had been given a thorough training and it was still possible to change to mechanical engineering where his red/green colour blindness wouldn't matter so much.

Coming round from his daydream James looked down again at his mangled legs and felt a throb of pain in the wounds. He gave a half-hearted smile: "To think, if I wasn't colour blind...if I'd never changed jobs then, I'd not be lying here now." Then with a shrug as if to chase away such useless thoughts, he turned on his side and tried once again to get off to sleep.

4
FAR FROM HOME

It was when he was twenty-two that James joined the Merchant Navy. He had qualified as an engineer in Peterhead and entered the navy as a junior engineering officer on the Moss-Hutchison Line. At last he was to be able to do what he had always wanted. He was to set off for the Mediterranean at once.

His parents were unhappy to see him go. Not that they had forbidden him - James' father had finally helped him to get the position. But they were worried about their son. During the last months of his apprenticeship he had become increasingly restless. He had been longing to get away from home - and from the church. Many of his friends were outside the assembly and he had been increasingly reluctant to go himself. The last thing they wanted was for him to join the Navy and be introduced to company and habits which they thought could only drag him down. His brother, Robert, although younger, was uninterested in the church. Would James go the same way?

Hoping that a spell away from home would be enough for James they had encouraged him to take a job in Chelmsford in Essex where they had friends. James had quickly agreed. As soon as he qualified he had been ready to leave.

Freedom had beckoned. "I can do what I like," thought

James. "I'll be living in digs. Nobody'll know the first thing about me. They'll not even have heard of Peterhead."

His initial plans had been thwarted, however, as soon as he had arrived in Chelmsford. Not only did he work with a man who belonged to a Brethren assembly in Chelmsford, this man actually hailed from Buckie, just along the coast from James' home town. He seemed to know everyone in Peterhead!

"It's not fair," demanded James. "He'll probably even make sure I go to church!" Although his father had given him contacts in the local assembly James was not keen to get too involved. He wanted to be his own man.

His initial ingratitude had soon been countered, however, by the chap's friendliness. He had introduced James to another Buckie family, the Hastings and they had invited him to their home and made him very welcome. Their four sons were good company and James soon made firm friends with them. For James was in need of friends. He had been surprised and embarrassed to find just how lonely and even homesick he felt for his parents and for Peterhead. After trying for so long to get away all he wanted to do was get back! He had found his digs very strained and formal. So different from his easy-going, open-doored home in Peterhead. And the job wasn't working out too well, either.

Soon he had moved in to lodge with the Hastings and he had been happier for a while, good cooking and cheerful company doing much to raise his spirits. Yet the old problems had remained. Much as he enjoyed his new friends' hospitality, he wasn't really his own boss. He wasn't as free had hoped. It was like a home from home - and had all the disadvantages to match.

So he had finally been allowed to join the Merchant Navy. He was to travel at last. There would be no homesickness this time, he assured himself. Each seven week voyage would be enjoyed to the full.

The year that followed saw James visiting the exciting and exotic places he had heard about for so long: Tripoli, in Libya where camels roamed the streets, men wore fez hats like Tommy Cooper, and women were shrouded in heavy, dark robes so only their eyes could be seen; the ancient sites of Thessalonica and Patmos; Istanbul, the city of a thousand, shining mosques but with back-streets as dirty and dark as engine oil; and Beirut, a beautiful city considered to be the 'crossroads of the Middle East' before it was destroyed by civil war.

The antipathy between Arabs and Israelis sometimes made travel between Israel and other countries difficult. If Israeli cargo was transported or if Israeli ships were used the Arabs would react angrily, even firing on the ships. Sight-seeing was always possible, however. The old chief engineer on board who had been on the Mediterranean run for as long as anyone could remember would give the new boys conducted tours - showing the seamier side of a city as well as its tourist attractions!

Lattakia in Syria was always a favourite. One of its mosques held a very eerie inhabitant - lying in its ancient grave clothes in a candle-lit chamber was an embalmed body said to be a thousand years old. But this sea port was also affected by internal political struggles. Swimming in the sea at the side of the ship one day rifle fire came shooting over their heads and went skimming into the swell.

"Get yourselves out of here!" yelled the captain and they swam round the ship as quickly as they could. The ship hastily left port and narrowly escaped involvement in a violent uprising which raged through the city.

James was in his element. With every port at which the ship docked there were new sites to see, new places to explore. And there were always plenty companions willing to join in any expeditions as soon as the work was done. Everywhere they travelled the men would seek out any party they could gate-crash or they would organise one themselves and James threw himself into the festivities. Although he knew inside that he was doing wrong it seemed all right - nobody really knew after all, he told himself. For a young man who had never tasted anything stronger than Irn Bru he quickly acquired a taste for beer and 'the hard stuff' which was sometimes the sole diet on the regular nights out. He even stopped being surprised at the numbers of girls who seemed only too happy to befriend a travelling sailor or at the philandering habits of his friends. He didn't have time to wonder: he was too busy joining in.

Even the work was enjoyable. There was always plenty to do and James felt that this was more the kind of work he wanted. The ship's engines were bigger than any he had worked on before and seemed a million miles away from the humble pickling plant he had received his training in. This was the 'big time' away from the familiar, away from the humdrum existence that had irked him for so long.

Often a voyage would take the crew into the waters of the Black Sea. Leaving Istanbul behind they would sail on beyond Bosporus. This port seemed to separate East and West. Beyond it everything changed. Great care was always taken when the ship visited the various countries and states of the U.S.S.R. which surround the Black Sea and the men were briefed on the definite 'do's' and 'don'ts': no photographs, no talking to the local people, no rowdy parties, don't attract attention, just do what you're told. Armed guards were seen all over the streets and at the harbour they would salute the men as they left the ship. On one occasion in Romania James disobeyed orders and tried to speak to a couple whom he met near the docks but although they responded initially they quickly slipped away. When James turned to see the cause of their disappearance he caught sight of an army guard observing him from nearby. He decided to disappear quickly himself!

After a year James decided to move to the Ben Line which ran steam ships through the tropics, carrying cargo to and from the Far East. He wanted to see as much of the world as possible and this trip, the first of many on the eastern run, would take him far beyond Suez for the first time. Travelling out through the Mediterranean, through the Red Sea and across the Indian Ocean, they would visit various ports in Malaysia, Singapore and Thailand. Then they would sail into Indonesia and the Philippines, up to Hong Kong and Japan before turning round and coming back through Suez again.

Although engineers were not known as officers, technically they were and on the trips to the Far East they were treated like lords. Eating with any first class passengers who might be on the ship they were fed four times a day and all the leisure activities were open to them. Deck tennis, quoits and other deck games were all part of the fun and if it got too hot at any time they could cool off in the pool. James would usually swim several times a day, especially as it got warmer. When the heat became more intense the relaxed atmosphere of the officers' lounge or the library was available to them. They would watch films or get up their own entertainment as they wished. It was a grand life.

Working in the engine rooms in the high temperatures of the Tropics and the Red Sea was always difficult. Often the thermometer would read 120 degrees as the machinery gave off its own heat in addition to the blazing sun outside. The engineers would work for four hours at a time in these conditions and they were glad to reach the fresh air again and a shaded spot on deck.

James' favourite shift was always from 4am to 8am as the sun began to rise in the east. Being much cooler he would have more energy to get on with his work. Sometimes after a shift during the night hours he would go onto the bridge and learn some navigation, determining their position by taking sightings of the moon and stars. It was fascinating to watch this being done and to learn the skill.

Often as few as a dozen or so Europeans would be aboard the vessel with the boat full of Chinese and Asian sailors. They were often friendly and would hour away the time telling ancient stories to one another. It wasn't always easy to understand what these stories were about but they were entertaining. James was soon taught by them how to eat with chopsticks and was instructed how to barter with the men who sailed out to the ship as it approached a port. This was quite a complicated affair. When they docked at Aden on the outward voyage, twelve days out to sea they were not permitted to go ashore as they were merely refuelling. Undeterred the 'bumboat men' paddled out in their tiny crafts and soon overran the boat, making the deck their store as they spread out their goods for sale or barter.

Bigamy was very common amongst the Chinese seamen and many had wives in different ports. Subsequently they had very large families and when they arrived in a port these men could invariably call on some member of their family to tend the boilers for them while they went on leave. Stripping the engines as they sat in port the officer on watch would often find some young nephew or grandson, grinning and nodding as he watched the gauges and valves move but not having any idea what he was supposed to be doing in response.

Having sailed in the Mediterranean and been initiated, as he saw it, into the lifestyle of a hardened sailor James had thought himself to be a real man of the world. As he journeyed further into the East he began to see that he was still very 'green'. He had been warned about the cities like Manila and Bangkok but he was unprepared for the immorality and danger on the streets. It was a part of every-day life, however, and he soon got used to the boat-loads of women who would pour onto the ship as it lay at anchor in a port. Tied up on the Bangkok river the bank would come alive at about two o'clock in the morning and whole night clubs seemed to descend on the ship. Lights would be set up, drinks would flow, music would start. Ropes would be thrown over the side to pull up the revellers and the party would begin. Drugs were sometimes to be found although the real traffic in them had not begun. These were things that would not be mentioned in the next postcard home!

When he was home on leave James spent more and more of his time out with his brother and his friends continuing the lifestyle he had learned at sea. Robert had rebelled early against their parents' way of life and beliefs. Now James joined him. The assembly now seemed so irrelevant to them both. Now and again James had sought out a church when he was in a port but more out of curiosity to see what it was like in another country rather than out of any desire to go to worship. He still felt some allegiance to Christianity. After a few drinks the subject of religion would invariably come up and he would defend it violently but with very vague reasoning. It had no meaning for him any more other than it represented part of his upbringing, something nostalgic but of no interest or importance. James knew that this greatly hurt his parents but as long as he was only at home briefly he hoped that it wouldn't be mentioned and nothing need be said.

James stayed with Ben Line for a few years but he still had a hankering to travel further afield. When he was at home on leave he felt restless and at a bit of a loss. Lots of his friends were getting married and settling down in their own homes, yet for him nowhere was home. He didn't want to be tied down and a few disastrous relationships had put him off marriage for sure! He had gone out with a girl in Aberdeen for quite a while, a radiographer, when he was at home but had shied off when it began to get serious. Girls were all right but the thought of getting married was just coming it a bit too strong!

Dipping into his Discharge Book which listed all his voyages and ports of call he tried to decide where he had yet to see. Canada? Antarctica?! Australia?

Without much more thought James signed up with Port Lines who carried general cargo outward via the Far East to Australia and New Zealand, and meat and dairy produce homewards across the Pacific through the Panama Canal and over the North Atlantic back to Britain. It was to be the first of six voyages around the world for James, a voyage which would change the direction of his life, suddenly and unexpectedly, and shape what would happen to him many years ahead.

Not long after James had set sail on M.V. *Port Auckland* with Port Lines and began work on the engines he contracted a form of dermatitis. He seemed to be allergic to something and his hands became red and sore. It made working really difficult and it wasn't long before they found what was causing the reaction. Somehow or another James had developed an allergy to engine oil. It was a disaster! How could he work as an engineer if he couldn't put his hands on anything? Was their another job on board that he could do?

At that time refrigeration on merchant vessels was being developed to enable the ships to carry perishable products on the long journey home. Much to James' relief the company offered to train James in it as he was no longer any use in the propulsion side of things. He felt pretty lucky that something had been found for him. He had begun to feel it was like his colour-blindness all over again - not able to do the job he was trained to do because of some trivial little defect. But at least he was learning a new skill. Perhaps he could make use of it sometime later on.

He was pleased not to have to leave the ship as he had settled in well and made new friends quickly. They seemed a good bunch with some younger boys amongst them as well. At the age of twenty-six James was amongst the older ones. They boasted to the young recruits. They would show these new boys a good time - just what being at sea was all about!

Yet even as he said these words James felt uneasy. Somehow this 'good life' of doing just what he liked was not all it was cracked up to be. It was really selfish for a start. James didn't seem to like himself very much any more, or like what he had become. There was also a young boy called Mervyn from Belfast there as junior engineer. He was only twenty-one and James sensed that much of the partying and drinking was new to him. Mervyn had been reluctant to join in initially although he was making up for lost time very quickly. Having seen him slip off to church now and again when they were in port James suspected that he had some Christian background like himself. James' conscience began to bother him - for Mervyn. As the young boy became more and more immersed in the 'other side of life' James could see himself as he had been only a few years ago - knowing that what he was doing was wrong but not wanting to be different. He had even wanted to forget all that he knew about falling away from the truth as if by forgetting about God he could say that God didn't exist. As he saw Mervyn starting to follow the same path that he had taken James knew that could never be true. He began to look hard at himself and it made him feel very uncomfortable.

"Brown, that's what you were like." He couldn't get it out of his head.

It was a Sunday when they docked at Manila. Once everything had been attended to James watched Mervyn head off into the city.

"He's off to church," thought James. "Probably a Roman Catholic. Maybe not. I could ask him. Maybe I could go with him."

Although he couldn't bring himself to join Mervyn he headed into the city himself and eventually found an Assembly of God church. There was a huge gathering of people and some of the service was in English. James half-listened. Half of his mind kept laughing at his own muddled state and the other half was desperate to hear what was being said. He arrived back at the boat very unsettled.

He had always known that he was heading the wrong way with his life. Now he saw the direction more clearly. Down. That was where he was headed - downwards. But now that he was thinking of turning around, he couldn't. He felt a strange mixture of defiance and impotence. Was it really that wrong? He wasn't much worse than any other? Yet he couldn't escape it. He had wanted his kicks out of life but he was hating himself as he was getting them. There was nothing he seemed able to do. The time for trying again seemed long gone.

Having trained as a barber James would often do a bit of hairdressing for his friends.

"How about a trim, Jim?" they would ask. "There'll be a beer or two in it for you." While they sailed towards Australia through the tropics the men would do anything to keep cool and James usually had his scissors ready. One afternoon James was cutting Mervyn's hair. The weather was bad and it wasn't easy for Mervyn to keep his head steady. A tropical storm was brewing and they joked about what Mervyn would look like by the end of it. 'A hurricane haircut' they could describe it as. They chatted a bit about what they would do in Adelaide and Sydney when they arrived but James was eager to find out about his young friend. But what could he say? Eventually he blurted out: "Do you...eh...go to church, like, Mervyn?" Mervyn looked up shyly at James.

"Now and again."

"Which church?" asked James wanting to ask more but not knowing how.

"Well, it's not one you'd have heard of," Mervyn replied cautiously.

"Oh, aye."

"Yeah. We're Elim Pentecostals at home."

James could hardly believe it. All the time he had been

in the Navy he had never met anyone who went to church, far less a Christian. And here was this young boy who belonged to the sister movement to the Assemblies of God. There and then James told Mervyn of his own upbringing. He was ashamed to see the amazement on the young man's face. "I don't look much like it now, eh?"

That night the seas were the worst that James had ever seen. Huge waves heaved the ship up and down. A gale was blowing and James huddled on his bunk in the cabin. He was miserable. And he was scared. The weather was bad but something more urgent was burning into his heart.

"What are you doing with yourself? Where are you heading?"

He thought of the choices he had been faced with as a young boy in the assembly at home and wondered if he had ever meant any of it.

"If I die tonight - say the ship goes down - where would I go?"

Even before the words had formed in his mind he was down on his knees on the cabin floor.

At that moment while the floor lurched in front of him James begged for forgiveness from his God. His conscience which had been so hardened had been touched and he knew where to turn. He needed a fresh start. He wanted to chose heaven and not hell to be his final destination just as he had done as a little boy but this time he did with his whole heart - no half measures, no short-cuts. He asked for a Saviour and nothing else would do.

The first port of call after that night was Adelaide. Again

Sunday had arrived. The moment he was free from his duties James headed into the city.

"Anyone got a 'phone book?" he had demanded. "I'm from Peterhead. I want to find a church."

5
HOMECOMINGS

I

Adelaide was good. Melbourne was better - but the best yet was reserved for when they docked in Sydney!

Sydney boasted the most beautiful harbour James had ever seen. In all his travels nothing took his breath away quite like the sight that met his eyes as their ship steamed in to port. He was mesmerised.

Deep blue sky met deep blue sea. The waters were dotted with hundreds of small crafts: delicate yachts with brilliant sails skimmed past squat, laden ferries; heavy carrier vessels and tall, graceful liners ploughed relentlessly towards the dock.

The quay itself stretched out beyond them in a great, circular sweep and on it stood the heart of the city. Its elegant buildings reached up from the water's edge and the 'Sydneysiders', as the population were known, coloured the busy streets.

Spanning the huge bay yawned the Sydney Harbour Bridge, arching majestically across the water. It pointed down like a giant finger to the growing shell of the new Opera House. Its sail-like roof was still under construction but promised to be as eye-catching as its proud surroundings.

Three rivers converged to form the harbour itself. They segmented the shoreline and smaller quays stretched up these tributaries for as far as James could see.

It was dazzling. Brilliant sunlight continually caught the edges of city buildings, reflecting off the shining steel of the Harbour Bridge, or the chrome funnel of a busy tug. They all glistened together like momentary stars. The whole scene was repeatedly sparked by a hundred natural, mercurial lights. The days spent in Sydney were the happiest James had known. Scores of untrodden beaches were waiting to be discovered beyond the city limits and he and his friends raced over them and into the sea, burning their feet on the scorching sand. The north Sydney coastline opened out into at least thirteen spectacular beaches, one leading into another as far as the eye could see. They visited towns and villages with outlandish names like Wooloomaloo and Wollongong and everywhere the people seemed easy-going and friendly.

Ever since that night when James had made his commitment to follow Jesus Christ he had looked up the local churches wherever they docked. He soon found that young Mervyn was only too happy to join him. He had been finding it difficult to be a solitary Christian and to stand out against the crowd. He just needed a little moral support to put aside his newly formed habits. Together they would head into the various cities trying to find somewhere to worship.

As they visited various ports James began to build up contacts in many of the churches. In Sydney the congregation which he and Mervyn first attended was always very hospitable and they found many among them who had emigrated or at least had relations in Britain. James even managed to find one or two who had originally come from the east coast of Scotland. In Brisbane he was made particularly welcome. A friend of James' father from his Musselburgh days, Jim Wallace, had founded an Assembly of God Bible School there and his widow, Meg ran an old people's home nearby. She treated James like a long lost son, delighting in spoiling him whenever he was in port.

Going to church voluntarily and enthusiastically was a new experience for James. He found that now he *wanted* to go - it was so different to his attitude to church at home. In those days reluctance to attend had turned into an unspoken resentment. But that was all over. Now, wherever he was, he found himself going to some church gathering almost every night of the week. There was so much for young people to do: Bible studies; barbecues; Rangers, a form of Christian adventure scouts; Ambassadors, another type of youth club. There were even summer camps which whole churches attended together over the Christmas holidays. James loved it all, making lots of new friends and learning a lot of what he felt he'd missed during his wild days. "If Mum and Dad could see me now..." he thought. He had written to tell them what had happened and he knew that they were delighted. They had never thought that the sea would have such a good effect on him - eventually!

James continued to work the Australia run for a couple of years, going home to Scotland or sometimes to Ireland every few months. Mervyn had left the sea after a year or so and James visited him in Belfast at the first chance he got. Mervyn had bought himself a sports car - an MG Midget - and they toured the Antrim coast in fine style together.

At this time James' shipping company amalgamated with another. The crew knew nothing about it. They had docked one morning in Sydney having been at sea for several weeks to find that in the interim their company, Port Lines, had become Atlas Lines! No jobs were lost, however. They merely changed their routes and their cargo. They now transported goods from Australia to Hong Kong and Japan. The Japanese seemed particularly fond of kangaroo meat and this was a common cargo. Often during the ten months that followed he would dock in both New Zealand and various ports in the islands off Japan's mainland.

Whenever they sailed from Australia, even when he was heading for Britain and home leave, James felt a strange longing to return. For a man who felt he had no particular roots and loved to move from place to place, he was curiously drawn to the country. It was as if his life had started again just as he had arrived for the first time - his new life. This wasn't the land of his birth but it was the land of his new birth, near enough, and he felt a real affection for the place. And he had made many friends there. Although he was never in port for long the ship would return regularly to the same cities and many in Sydney and Brisbane welcomed him into their homes. And he loved the relaxed pace of life. The sports and games were just what he liked most - swimming, water-skiing, surfing - and the climate was glorious. There was no winter to speak of and he thought how easy it would be to get a job there. Here he was, a refrigeration engineer, in one of the warmest countries of the world. Nobody was too worried about qualifications either. Australia was a young country that seemed to be crying out for new blood and if you had something to offer they would give you a try. They wouldn't tell you to come back in a few years with some diplomas under your belt like they did in Britain. He liked the people too. They were sometimes accused of being blunt and even brash but to James they were straightforward and uncomplicated. It didn't matter whom you knew or who knew you. They took you on face value. It had *never* been like that in Peterhead.

During those days the first seeds of a growing plan were planted in James' mind. He thought for the first time of settling down. Emigration was being actively encouraged by both British and Australian governments. It would be easy to do. And the more he heard about it the more promising it seemed. He even discovered that he could get all his documentation *and* his passage for as little as ten pounds! It was certainly worth thinking about.

In both New Zealand and Japan he was able to find somewhere to worship. In New Zealand he found several Assembly of God churches and in the North Island he was able to meet with Maori Christians too. He loved the Maori hymnsinging. They had their own words and slow lilting tunes almost like Hawaiian love songs. It was very relaxed. 'Tomorrow is as good as today' was their motto. James had thought that the Australians were laid back but these New Zealanders made them seem like regular speedmerchants!

He wondered how they managed to keep awake in church with the slow, soothing music and the lazy atmosphere. But maybe that didn't matter either, he thought!

Japanese churches were quite different. James went to several, mainly through a missionary contact he had made in Australia: Marie Smith had spent many years out in Japan and was currently running an orphanage for 'G.I. kids'. She had been spending a furlough in Australia with Meg Wallace while James had been visiting and she had invited him to visit her should he ever land in Kobe where she worked. He took her at her word and was not only shown round the tourist attractions in the area but was also given introductions to a number of her friends throughout Japan. Soon he was meeting her contacts both in Tokyo and on the several islands which form the southernmost tip of the country.

James arrived during one voyage at a church in Kita-Kyushu on the island of Kyushu. This is one of the larger islands in the south. Marie Smith had contacted her friend, Pastor Rikimaru, and this Japanese minister was expecting James to arrive.

James found the Japanese people to be extremely courteous and gentle. With slow measured movements they conveyed a certain grace and dignity in all they did - very different from the Aussies! As he entered the church in Kita-Kyushu he was greeted very politely and led decorously towards a place where he might sit. The congregation all sat on the floor or on cushions, the women on one side and the men on the other. James took his place beside them. He felt very conspicuous being the only westerner there. There were about forty in the congregation, all Japanese, and very few spoke any English. Yet with smiles and friendly gestures they made him feel very welcome. He spoke no Japanese but he was at least able to hum through some of the hymns: they sang the first one to the Scottish tune of 'Annie Laurie'! He began to feel quite at home.

James received a shock, however, when he was asked to the front to address the congregation. He was terrified. He had never spoken about his faith in this sort of setting, far less preached to anyone. He stumbled through a brief speech and was thankful that it was being translated: that would make it seem a bit longer, he hoped! As he stood there he had no idea what they thought of it although his listeners' heads nodded gravely at all he said. The nods crept round the church like a great hypnotising wave. He hoped 'nodding' in Japanese meant 'yes'.

Pastor Rikimaru invited James into his home that day and he and his family were extremely kind. So polite were they that James watched carefully so that he would not make some social faux-pas: they were so gracious that he was sure that they would not wish to have to ask him to do anything. He therefore removed his shoes as the family did on entering the house and stepped carefully through the light sliding doors. The house was of the traditional Japanese style with bamboo walls and the oriental, curving roof. Inside he sat tentatively on the delicate tatamic matting which covered the floor. It was like interwoven raffia and would have been easily damaged by shoes or boots. As he couldn't speak the language he just sat and smiled at what he thought were appropriate moments. He seemed bound, however, for some dreaded mistake and when he was asked if he would like a bath the stage was set.

James accepted the offer very readily. The weather had been quite cold and he thought a bath might warm him up. He was shown into a small room. In the middle of the floor was a round, sunken pool. It was already filled to the brim with steaming water. As she left him the pastor's daughter who spoke some English explained what he should do.

"You must know that this is a bath, Japanese-style. It is not to wash yourself but to relax. Before you go in you must be clean." She pointed to a shower head at the other side of the room.

James took his shower and then stepped into the pool. He slid cautiously downwards until he was immersed up to his chin in the piping hot water. It was wonderfully soothing. Rather like a still water jacuzzi it made his muscles relax and he could have dozed off if he hadn't been careful. He just lay back and let himself soak.

After about a quarter of an hour of this luxury James thought he should rejoin the family. Reluctantly he clambered out, leaning back in to pull out the plug. The water drained away as he dried himself and as he pulled on his clothes the last of it gurgled down the plughole.

With a great rasping splutter, steam suddenly began to billow out of the plughole. Then, like one of the hot water geezers he had seen in New Zealand huge columns of hot steam whooshed up into the air, quickly filling the room. James didn't know what to do.

Just then Pastor Rikimaru came bursting into the room. He looked panic-stricken. The lightly built house shook with the unexpected violence of his dash to the bathroom. Even the walls were shaking. He sped towards the bath and fumbled frantically for the plug. He pushed it into its hole before rushing out again. James was mystified. He had no idea what was going on. A moment later his host reappeared with buckets of cold water which he threw into the bath with a great splash and continued doing so until it was full. Unable to explain himself with his limited English vocabulary Pastor Rikimaru merely smiled at James through the steam when he finished. James wondered what disaster seemed to have been narrowly averted. Guiltily he wondered what he had done.

He soon learned that the steam had poured into every room of the house. Somehow he seemed to have barely avoided wrecking the Rikimaru's entire central heating and hot water system!

"You must never pull the plug from the pool," the daughter explained afterwards. "There is a fire always burning beneath the pool to heat the water. If you let the water out the fire might blow up the pool."

"Do you never change the water then?" asked James incredulously.

"We never need to empty the tub," she replied. "Everyone is clean when they go in so we just remove any scum with a jug and pour in some more cold water. It is just like a little swimming pool, really."

When he returned to the ship James told the boys about

it. They always marvelled how he managed to meet so many of the local people whenever he went ashore. He always seemed to have some contact who would give him lavish hospitality. Often James would invite his friends to go with him but they were wise to him.

"Don't go with that man," they would say. "Okay, so you'll get a fancy dinner and maybe a guided tour but watch out - he always ends up at a church!"

The banter was lighthearted, however. It had been difficult to make his friends understand what had happened to him and why he had changed overnight, but now they seemed to realise that this was the way James was and they grudgingly respected him for it. Perhaps directed to James through this teasing a few young boys sought him out, finding themselves in the same predicament that he had been in. James hoped that he could help them in some way. He could certainly recognise their difficulties and he knew how tempting it all was. Maybe, he thought, he could demonstrate simply that there was another way.

II

After ten months with the new company James had decided what he wanted to do. He loved the sea. His job had given him the chance to see a lot of the world and that had always been his ambition. But now that he had done that his thoughts were turning elsewhere. It seemed crazy that he was always sailing away from the place he had grown to love most - Australia. Why not live there for good?

When James decided anything he was never long in doing something about it and he informed Atlas Lines immediately. As soon as his notice was completed he was off. A few goodbyes were regretfully made; a few last photographs were taken. But James was never one to think twice. They docked in London in September. He had three months paid leave in his pocket. He would go home to Peterhead and sort out the documentation and as soon as Christmas had come and gone, he would be away. It was 1968. James was twenty-nine and he had been at sea for the best part of six years.

After the initial reunions and when he had set the emigration plan in motion, James thought he should look around for a temporary job. Sometimes being known in a community has its uses and he soon began work in a local fish processing plant. There was an ice-making factory attached to it and his expertise in this line was appreciated. The business was a family concern. Several of the Buchan family worked directly in it but when James joined the firm a difficult, delicate problem had arisen amongst them.

The Buchans were Brethren people and they were of the 'exclusive' or 'close' persuasion. This meant primarily that they excluded from the Sacrament of the Lord's Supper those who were not of the same - even identical - beliefs as themselves. From this one standard several other decrees were added but they were typical of exclusive Brethren assemblies everywhere. However, some in Peterhead had gone much further than was usual through the teaching of one of the leaders, Jim Taylor. Various edicts were pronounced by this man concerning the practice of the membership. How they should behave was increasingly spelled out to them. Many of these decrees concerned how the membership should separate themselves from those who were not of their number. They must live a separate existence. It quickly became difficult for many to continue with their family life, their jobs and any interests which might not be directly appointed by the assembly. Why such didactic control was possible is perhaps due to the nature of Peterhead itself and the surrounding villages. For as long as anyone could remember the strongly-felt religious fervour of the area had affected everyday life: these communities had long been accustomed to the impact of personal beliefs upon industry, education, local politics and so on.

The latest edict was very problematic for the Buchans. Jim Taylor had announced that not only was Sunday to be observed as a day of rest in common with all other denominations, but Saturday was also to be kept as the Lord's Day. Essentially this meant that no work could be carried out on Saturday *or* on Sunday. Church meetings would be held on both days. The firm was in a real quandary. The fishermen returned at the weekend and always deposited fish - and therefore required ice - throughout Saturday. In both sides of the business it was their busiest day of the week. Yet if the Buchans were to remain in their assembly they would have to stop production. What could they do?

Not long after he began working for them James was approached by the Buchan family. He knew the ice-making business. He was not involved in any other venture. More important, he was not involved in the Brethren disputes. Would he not take it over?

James had no hesitation in turning this offer down. His heart was set on Australia. As far as he was concerned he was merely putting in time until he could leave. He had to say no. However, from this situation James' father became involved. He had set up his own hairdressing business but was keen to try something else. Perhaps with a little tuition from James he could pick up the basics of the business within a few months. He wanted to give it a go anyway. Before long James' father had sold up and had bought a quarter share of the Buchan enterprise. He would run the place under his own name although they left capital in it. As long as the Buchans were not seen to be involved in a Saturday-working company, they were all right.

It soon became evident that James would be able to help out his father for rather longer than he had thought. Just as his emigration papers were being completed one unforeseen development occurred. He wouldn't delay his departure to take over a business but, well...this was different.

It was Christmas and lots of parties for the young people were taking place throughout the churches. James went to a few although he was beginning to find himself amongst the oldest there. It was at a party in nearby Cairnbulg that James met Margaret for the first time.

Although they had never actually spoken James had been teased about Margaret on many occasions. His pals had described them as 'the perfect couple' - 'just right for each other' - but James had shrugged them off. Yet he noticed her as soon as she came in the door.

"Who's the dark haired quine that's just come in?" he asked the folk with whom he was sitting.

"Who? Oh, Margaret? That's Margaret Buchan. You know her, don't you? She's in the Cairnbulg assembly."

"I remember the name," James murmured. He was suddenly embarrassed, knowing what was coming.

"We'll have to introduce you. Now she would be just the girl for you! A lovely Christian girl. Mind you, who's that she's got with her? I've not seen him around."

James was thankful that they were distracted from the matchmaking that was clearly about to take place. But he also wondered who Margaret's companion could be. He watched them as they came into the room.

"She's pretty, right enough," he thought to himself. "Funny that we've never met. Trust me to see her just when I'm about to leave. It would have been good to go out sometime. But then - looks like she's got a date already. Probably been going out a while."

Before long his friends had sat Margaret down beside them and they were introduced. The man who was with her came too. He was called Peter Cordiner and as they talked it turned out that he knew James' father. Peter came from Boddam, a village nearby but he was studying through in Aberdeen University. They were quickly chatting about mutual family friends and what it was like to be back home.

Yet as they spoke James was thinking more of Peter's female friend sitting beside him rather than any of his father's cronies! It was quickly clear that Margaret and Peter had just come as friends to the party together: they weren't going out at all.

James' Australian friends had often tried to match him up with various girls. They would tell him in their usual blunt manner that if he was going to emigrate he would need not just a girlfriend but a wife. James had said little. On one occasion he had actually met up with someone in London while he was on leave who had been *recommended* to him but it had come to nothing. He would marry an Australian, he said, just to keep them quiet. But marriage was too big a step for him. He had been stung more than once and he was very wary of becoming entangled in any relationship just now. No domestic ties or cares. He liked just being a free agent. He would be leaving in a few weeks anyway. But, yet, here was Margaret...would a few nights out hurt?

James asked Margaret out that night and they seemed to get on straight away. Before he knew what he had said James was arranging another date.

"But there's nothing in it," he said. "Just a few nights out."

"Oh, yes," agreed Margaret and they both seemed happy. So they had another date, and another, and another. A couple of weeks went by and James was becoming aware that Margaret was never far from his mind. They saw each other often but it was still agreed that there was 'nothing in it'. Yet as James filled out more emigration forms and waited every day to hear that his passage had been cleared he was not as happy as he had thought he would be. Somehow it was hard to leave Margaret out of his plans.

By the fifth week James was completely mixed up. What was happening? What did Margaret think? Should he say something? If he didn't he felt like he would burst!

Walking home with Margaret on Friday night that week James' steps became slower and slower. They were strolling along the esplanade in Fraserburgh and the winter wind was blowing in from the sea. But he wasn't noticing. Neither of them were talking much. James was thinking hard. More forms had arrived that morning to finalize his departure date. It was now or never - he had to speak up.

"Margaret," he rushed, "have you ever been abroad?" He felt he was being very bold!

"I was on a trip to Scarborough once," she replied. This was not the response James had been looking for. He tried again.

"Would you ever like to go abroad?" he asked. He mentioned some friends from the area who had left to go overseas.

"Well," she paused, "I could never go on my own."

He watched her face closely. Her head was bent forward and she wouldn't look at him. She was blushing. James wondered if he was blushing too.

"And how about going abroad with someone else?"

"That would depend who it was, wouldn't it?"

"Would you ever...em...think about going abroad ...with... with me?"

"How do you mean?" she murmured. "I could never go just like, you know...well...single."

"Would it make any difference, then, if we were

married?" The words were out before he even thought about it.

Margaret didn't know where to look. "That," she said, "would make all the difference in the world."

What they had said sank in slowly. James was stunned. What was Margaret saying? What had he said? What had they done?

"Margaret," he stammered, "I...I think you had better have a week or so to think this over..."

The proposal, whoever made it, was in February on only their fifth night out and they were married in July. Emigration was still part of the plan but papers had to be swiftly changed and new requests submitted. James and Margaret agreed together that should either of them ever want to come home, for any reason, they had only to say. Yet in September they were ready to set off. Margaret had to leave behind the family from whom she had never been apart and James felt very responsible for her happiness. He would be the only person she would know once they left Scotland.

III

The following are a selection of the letters sent home by James from Australia.

4/10/69
Dear Ma and Da,
I hope you got our first letter and know that we have survived the journey and have arrived! That first week was

brilliant - like having an extended holiday. We've really got down to all the arrangements now, though.

We've managed to get our own place in Sydney. It's a flat in the suburbs, Marrickville, and Margaret likes it fine. We're going to move in straight away.

It'll be good to get into our own place although the Thompsons have been great. The fact that he's the pastor has had some advantages. We've been able to meet lots of folk from the church so there's hardly been time to be homesick. We've had transport too - being driven about in Bill's fancy car. I remember when I met him first all those years ago when I docked in Sydney looking for a church. He rolled up then in a swanky Desoto like something out of a film. He's still as weird as ever. I think he's got what's called megalomania or something. It's apparently some medical condition where he thinks he's a superstar. He's got a lot worse since I was here last. He's been chartering planes and buying lots of really showy, expensive stuff. He'll be bankrupt before he knows it. His poor wife must be at her wits end.

Anyway, back to the flat. It's weird thinking that we've got to buy everything for it. Margaret's got a list but we just keep adding to it. The daily papers here have lots of adverts for second hand stuff, like, so we'll be all right. Bill Thompson's daughter has been great, lending us some stuff, like a table and a couple of chairs, and plates and cutlery enough for two. We won't be doing much entertaining for a while! We're not stuck for work either. The Sydney Morning Herald is a massive newspaper - 105 pages - and it has 50 *pages full of jobs! It's pretty much a case of picking and choosing. Margaret's fixed up already in a stockbroker's office and I'm starting with an engineering firm. They're making steel for the Opera House that I told you about. Looks like it'll be okay but if something comes up in refrigeration I'll probably go for it.*

We went along to the Petersham Assembly of God last Sunday and I met more old friends. Do you remember David Wirtz I used to talk about? We had a fine time. Poor Margaret, though. She's getting tired of being introduced and being told that they thought I'd never get hitched! They make out that she's some sort of wonder woman. You never know what these Aussies are going to say. They come out with anything!

It'll be getting warm here soon so we'll be heading for the beach before long. Think of us as you dig out the winter woollies!

Let me know how the business is going, Dad.

God bless,
Love to everyone,
James and Margaret

5/12/69
Dear Ma and Da,
Well, we've bought a car - a second hand Mazda. It's not really in the Bill Thompson class but you really need a car here. We're thinking of going up to Brisbane to see Meg Wallace - you remember - Jim's widow. It'd be great to see

her again, and of course she is itching to meet Margaret!

We'll meet up with Ruth Stephen there too. Do you remember she came out a few years back from Cairnbulg? She's working in the old folk's home that Meg runs. She actually visited us the other day with some friends of hers. They were heading for Adelaide for their summer holidays and spent the day with us to break the journey. What a panic Margaret was in! Our trunks - the things coming by boat - you know, the ones with all the wedding presents, plates and dishes and linen and stuff, hadn't arrived, and we didn't even have enough plates to serve them their food on. She wanted things to be half-decent - didn't want anyone, especially someone from home, to know that we only had a couple of knives and forks to our name! Anyway, Margaret was saying it was a miracle - the trunks arrived the day before Ruth and her friends appeared. Amazing, eh? We had a really good time with them. Oh, and Ruth says that Mrs Wallace asks to be remembered to you.

You'd hardly believe the number of folk we've met from round about Peterhead. Did I tell you about the man next door to us in our flat - Bill York? Aye - he's English right enough but he was stationed in Peterhead during the war, at the Cairnbulg airfield! It was really weird. He recognised our accents and was asking about Peterhead and all as soon as we met - like "Does the local train still run from Fraserburgh to Cairnbulg?" - He used to take it every day, like. Another man along the way is Scottish and guess where he comes from? - Aberdeen! It's a small world, sure enough. See, Ma, we're not really that far away.

The rest of the neighbours are a mixed bunch. And I mean mixed! It seems that we're in a Greek district and nearly everyone is Greek. No wonder they couldn't understand us! Greeks work in just about all the local shops and the post office and everything. Really weird! We'll be getting Greek accents next. Mind you, there's not much chance of that with all the other folk in our block. There are eighteen flats and there are Germans, Dutch, English, Lebanese, and of course, Scots! Pretty varied. They seem fairly friendly, though. I suppose they've emigrated too and can remember what it was like.

Work is going well. Margaret has been a bit homesick, what with Christmas coming up and all but she's okay.

Better go, be in touch,

All our love,
James and Margaret

30/1/70
Dear Ma and Da,
Well, Christmas has come and gone and it's still as hot as ever here. Even the nights are hot - 75 and 80 degrees.
The 'in' thing here is to have barbecues and we were at one over the holidays to do with the assembly. It was great - different from anything Margaret had seen, anyway! They hired one of the harbour ferries and shipped everyone over to one of the islands in Sydney harbour. We had it all to ourselves. What a crowd were there! There must have been about thirty different countries represented apart

from anything else and loads of these folks got up and did some singing in their own languages or played instruments. One chap in the church, Ross Smith, is a brilliant saxophone player - and singer for that matter - and he entertained us too. Lights were strung up all over the place. It was a lovely sight. And kind of balmy, too - really peaceful and warm. And the Aussies certainly know how to feed themselves well. They could show a Peterhead 'social' a thing or two! Steaks and hot dogs cooking in the open air, loads of fancy salads set out on trestles and weird sauces to go with everything.

Philip Duncan, the old pastor at Petersham, is a great guy. He turned up in one of those wild Hawaiian shirts. He looked really funny. He must be seventy if he's a day. He's so kinda dumpy and - well, fatherly that he gave us all a good laugh with his trendy gear!

He's a really fine man. He's awful for teasing, though, especially Margaret. She never knows when to take him seriously. The other day in church he handed her a wee parcel as he passed her going up the aisle. "That'll maybe stop you feeling homesick," he said and gave it to her. She was too embarrassed to open it there and then and pushed it under the seat. It's a wonder that she didn't smell it, though - it was a pair of Aberdeen kippers, vacuum packed and transported to one of the big stores in Sydney! It was a real taste of home. We sat outside in the sun and ate them like a picnic, thinking of the rain and snow at home.

Anyway, give us your news when you write. Poppy and Horry - those relations of Margaret's that we tracked down in Sydney - send their love. We see them every now and again on an evening. They give us all the 'gen' from home, being in touch with folk up the coast and round about Peterhead.

God bless you both,
Love from
James and Margaret

6/10/70
Dear Ma and Da,

It was good to hear from you. Business sounds like it's going well, Dad. If the disputes in Aberdeen really come to anything like you mentioned Peterhead could be docking a lot more fish so it seems like it's on the increase.

Thanks too for the Sievwrights address. The holidays are coming up and we plan to go over to Tasmania soon so we'll be able to visit them in Melbourne on the way.

We've got another car for the trip to hold us all - an Austin 1800. It should be big enough but we don't know how reliable it is. It plays up sometimes and is prone to burning as much oil as petrol. We're just hoping that we won't get stuck. Tasmania's a bit uninhabited, so they say.

We've been meeting more folk at church. There's a meeting on Saturday night - Christ's Ambassadors - for folks of our age and a bit younger and we have a great time.

The creepie crawlies have been really getting to Margaret. There are hundreds of those Christmas beetles about just now. They look a bit like big ladybirds. They cling to your skin and although they don't do any harm, she hates them. They're quite big, about the size of a five pence piece, and have claws that get a grip of you. I've been telling her to worry about the worse things like black widow spiders but somehow that makes her worse!

We thought we'd make a tape sometime - like speaking a letter instead of writing it. You know how bad I am at getting round to writing. Margaret says if I have a new gadget to play with like a microphone and a recorder perhaps I'll keep in touch better! See if you can get hold of a tape recorder, too, Dad and we'll make one sometime.

I'd better go. Sorry to hear that you're feeling poorly again, Ma. Let us know what the doctor says about it in your next letter.

Love from
James and Margaret

12/1/71
Dear Ma and Da,
We just got back the other week from Tasmania with the Mitchell couple from church. Did everyone get our postcards? We met up with the Sievwrights as well. In fact, that was quite a laugh. We arrived in Melbourne on the Sunday and landed on them having arrived too late for the morning service. We meant just to say hello and maybe have a bite to eat but Harry invited us to stay the night before we met the ferry. When we said we could hardly do that he thought we didn't like his house! He asked us if there was anything wrong with it! And the thing was - it was just like a palace! It had a bathroom off all the bedrooms and was really beautiful. We couldn't have got better at a hotel if we'd tried.

THE ONLY WAY TO WALK

The ferry over to Tasmania was fine. I wasn't sure how Margaret would like the crossing but it was great to be back at sea again - a good feeling. The place itself is really weird. Pretty wild and uninhabited with tiny villages dotted about here and there. Can you imagine? There are hardly any trees and no grass. Apparently the sulphur mines have burnt the vegetation. Even the roads were rough and ready - just dirt tracks most of the time. We kept expecting a wild west stagecoach to come round the next bend. Even Queenstown was like that. You could just imagine cowboys galloping into town and having a shoot out in front of the local saloon!

We had a great time, though. It funny to see the place where they manage to grow all those apples that we used to transport everywhere. I don't know how they grew at all. There must be apple trees somewhere but we certainly didn't see them.

We were at a wedding too since we got back and we're invited to another at the end of the year. That'll be our fourth since we got here. It seems weird that they get married round Christmas time but I suppose it's natural, being their summer and all. This wedding was different from most Aussie weddings which have a buffet and you just stand around chatting. This one had a proper sit-down meal - after the hors d'oevres out on the lawn! Very fancy. It was really lovely though with speeches and 'cutting the cake' like we do at home. Write soon and God bless.

We think of you and pray for you often.

Love,

James and Margaret

11/71

Dear Ma and Da,

Did I tell you that I'd taken a new job again? Margaret nearly had a fit when I came home and told her! But it's worked out really well. It pays $10 more a week and the guy has got some British connections. We got on really well at the interview. And it's to do with refrigeration. Margaret was more worried that it was my fourth job in the last couple of years. She said she didn't know what she'd tell her mother! I don't think her Mum got over Margaret telling her she had a new job herself with that transport company and was working with lots of Lebanese women. I think they are wondering what I've done to their little daughter.

The atmosphere in my new office is really English. The firm's main office is in Guildford in Surrey and they really pride themselves on being British even although the Australian twang is as broad as anything. They think to be Scottish is one stage even better so they've been really friendly.

I have been given an awful lot of work to do, though. They wanted me to start work the day of my interview there was so much to do! Even so, they never let work get in the way of their 'leisure time'. They are all very relaxed about life. Recently I was so busy I volunteered to go in on a Saturday. When Mr Grosvener, the boss, saw me he was shocked - said I should be down at the beach!

We had a pleasant surprise a while back when my old ship mate, Merv, knocked at our door! He had flown into Sydney with his big VC10 jet. He is a 1st Pilot Officer now with *BOAC*. He hasn't changed a bit, though. He's married now - to an air hostess. They live near Oxford somewhere. Her folks are Methodists. He said he would bring her out to Sydney for a holiday to see us.

I've started going to night classes to do with work - three nights a week. There's a pile more to learn on refrigeration. It's really great. I'm determined to learn all the ins and outs.

It was good to hear all your plans, Da. The ideas about a new factory sound good. There's certainly a need for another ice plant and it sounds as if more and more work could be coming to Peterhead with that Wharfies strike in Aberdeen. Those fish-landers are going to find themselves up the creek. They'll be so busy working their rigid five day week they'll not be able to stop the boats coming up the coast to land their catches at places like Peterhead.

The process you have at present is pretty crude, though and I think you'll be needing a much higher production rate. Some of these night classes have got me thinking about it all and I bet you could import some gear and expertise. The Scandinavians are certainly at the head of the field. If the Harbour Authority are willing to provide the jetty and the finance seems to be available you really could be rolling, Da.

Before you ask, though, we're not thinking of coming home although we have talked of it a bit. We do miss you a lot and if I was ever to come back the Ice Company sounds ideal, but - well, life's good here for now anyway. We're really happy.

Church is going well and we are involved with a Ranger

group. There are a lot of young folk and they've been arranging weekends away round Sydney and into the bush. Fairly adventurous.

Anyway, I've got to go. We think of you and pray for you all the time.

God bless,
Love to you both,
James and Margaret

IV

It was after they had been in Australia for about two and a half years that the letter came from James' father bringing the news that his mother was gravely ill.

5/3/72
...Ma is very low...cancer in the brain...inoperable tumour...advanced stage...she mentions you often...we thought you should know.

That night James and Margaret went to Poppy and Horry's to phone home to Peterhead. The resulting conversation left no doubt in their minds. James' father had not asked them to come home but he had not protested when they had mentioned it. They would pack up and set off for home straight away.

Within an incredible three weeks they were home. Having decided together what they would do James set in about the arrangements in his usual rapid style. They got rid of their apartment, sold their furniture and gave up their jobs. James could not be tempted purely by any business deal with his father but the news of his mother brought him running home. He had always been so close to his mother that he wanted to see her. She died two months after they returned.

Before they had left for Australia James and Margaret had agreed that should either of them want to go home at any stage, they would go. Although she had been homesick Margaret had said very little. She knew how much their new way of life meant to her husband. But, somehow, this news made all the difference. When they left Sydney so suddenly to go home both Margaret and James knew that this was for good. They wouldn't be going back to live there. They were returning to Peterhead and there they would stay. There were many friends left behind in Sydney and elsewhere at the other side of the world but it was a strangely easy decision to make. With his mother gone James' father would need him, he felt. It was right for him to support his father now. And home was home. The call to return had been unexpected - a big shock - but when it came it changed everything. It drew them home - to stay.

The years that followed were good to James and Margaret. All his father's talk of the ice business and all his planning paid off and soon James joined him in the Peterhead Ice Company. It seemed purpose built for him and his experience was put to good use. Huge loans were forthcoming and permission to build their factory and strengthen the jetty was received. The new imported equipment was very heavy and the Model Jetty, named after the 'Model Doss House' that had been situated opposite it many years ago, had to be restructured to take the weight. The process they introduced was new to Scotland and overnight it increased production from a meagre ten tonnes a day to seventy. It continued to increase. As the fish merchants and fishermen began to use Peterhead more and more with industrial action restricting landings in Aberdeen business boomed - it was a real success. James and his father paid off all their loans in five years. And family life was happy too. There was more than Margaret and himself to think about now: Fiona had been born a year after they had come home and Graham had arrived three years later.

Again James' life had been changed suddenly and unexpectedly. With one phone call his Australian plans for his future were over. Yet he did not think that some cruel, indiscriminate hand of Fate was playing with his life. He knew it was God's hand that was shaping him and was mapping it out for him. James had always been told, even as a young boy, that he was like his mother. For many years throughout her various illnesses she had remained confident that what was given to her was part of God's perfect plan. She also knew that because of that her God would see her through and would direct her whatever happened to her. As James settled down to the life at home his faith was similar. God's plan was perfect. If God was in control of events James had no need to worry. If God wanted him back in Peterhead for some reason then that was okay. He was safer in God's hands than anyone else's.

It was this man, therefore - successful factory owner and contented family man, a man who thought his life was beginning, at last, to be settled and predictable after all his wandering and all the changes - it was this man who strode briskly along the jetty and into the factory for one last check on that silent September night.

6

STEPS TO RECOVERY

"How much further?"

"Just a few more steps, Mr Brown. One more turn down the bars and then back to the ward."

"That's what you said last time," James gasped trying to raise a smile. His hands felt as raw as his stumps from clinging so tightly to the parallel bars.

"Save your energy for walking and you'll soon be done," came the quick reply.

"Bully!"

For days now James had been working with the physiotherapist in the gym, trying to build up his strength and endure the pain of walking on his 'tin legs'. He was determined to make a success of whatever he was given but these first legs were great bulky things made out of aluminium with huge feet on them. There seemed to be very little padding and he was given thick, woollen stockings to protect his wounds. But they seemed to make little difference. Having to press all his weight onto his swollen, tender stumps and then into the hard unyielding metal, *and then to walk* on them was about as much as James could take. As he arrived at the end of his final stretch between the parallel bars he said as much to the physiotherapist. Beads of sweat were standing out on his forehead and his whole body was quivering as he lay back on the mat on the floor. She unfastened the clumsy limbs trying to encourage him now that the exercise was all over.

"That's the furthest you've walked, though," she smiled. "The longer you manage to keep going, the quicker you can get out of that wheelchair for good."

James had been in hospital for over a month and he was getting frustrated with it all. To anyone who knew of his injuries he was making miraculous progress, getting a wheelchair in three weeks and his first legs in four, even getting home for his first weekend only twenty days after his accident. But to James who could never stay in one place or sit still unless he was asleep, all this waiting and hanging about was endless!

He found the nights particularly long. Although he was continually offered sleeping tablets he was reluctant to take too many of them and was consequently awake for much of the night. It was then that the pain would become intolerable with nothing to distract him but the steady, monotonous snoring and heavy breathing of his slumbering companions. Often during these weary hours he would hoist himself into his wheelchair and trundle up the ward to chat to the night staff at the nurses station. This was strictly forbidden. The nurses lived in dread of the Nursing Officer coming into the ward and finding James out of bed, having a cup of tea with them. Occasionally she would turn up and the nurses would jump to their feet, throwing on their cardigans which they were supposed to wear at all times but never did. James knew when to make himself scarce.

"Just heading to the bathroom, ladies. No, no, I can manage. I wouldn't want to keep you from your work!"

Then with as straight a face as he could pull he would wheel himself out of sight before anything could be said.

He had been given the wheelchair at the beginning of the third week. What excitement there had been. He was like a young teenager who had just passed his driving test. What a release from being trapped in his bed! Up and down the ward he went, getting faster and faster. His left leg was still in plaster to keep it straight and it stuck out in front of him on a support. He was quite a hazard to avoid.

Soon he had discovered the lifts and visited other wards where he knew a couple of patients. Although he tired quickly he couldn't get enough of his new independence.

He was very nervous of the lifts, however. It was the only way of getting about so he felt he had to use them yet he was strangely afraid. He had never been bothered by lifts before his accident - he wasn't claustrophobic or scared of getting stuck inside - but it was the automatic doors that now made him panic every time he had to go through them. With his legs sticking out in front of him he was terrified of being squashed between the doors as they closed. He would grip the wheels of his chair with his fists, willing himself to push them round so he could get to the door as it opened and then dash through. It was a strange sensation which he never understood. Memories seemed mixed up with his dreams and his nightmares so that they all churned away inside him even throughout the day. "It's irrational, man," he would tell himself. "Get a grip!" But it was no use. Whether it made sense or not, he was still scared stiff.

James had been warned to expect feelings like these - and much worse. On ward rounds when the consultant orthopaedic surgeon, Mr Mills, would be accompanied by various other doctors, nurses and physiotherapists they would discuss his mental attitude as often as his physical state. James always found Mr Mills very understanding. Perhaps the surgeon recognised James' strong and determined spirit which his patient would need to fight the difficulties which would inevitably lie ahead. He always encouraged James to be positive. But the others were more cautious. They would talk of 'not going too fast', 'pushing back your discharge further than ever' and 'terrible depression'. Once when they found him signing some papers to do with the business they became quite irate. 'The man's a work-aholic,' they said, '...heading for a mental breakdown'. It seemed like scaremongering to James.

"What's wrong with getting going again as quickly as possible?" he would ask bluntly. "Why am I going to go off my head?"

James never suffered the breakdown that so many anticipated for him. He maintained that the promise from God that he had received while he sat alone after the accident was enough for him. He had been given that to hold onto. He was being protected, whatever had happened to him already. It was up to him, therefore, to keep his end up...to do his utmost to recover...to fight all the difficulties with whatever strength he was given. He did not feel that this was unusual. He was just getting on with the job in hand as he had always done.

Yet on one occasion he began to think that the threatened breakdown had happened. He was lying in the ward with the curtains drawn round his bed. A nurse, a coloured girl who often changed his dressings had just finished this task and she was clearing away the soiled bandages at the end of his bed. Slowly a strange feeling was creeping over James as he lay there, not saying a word. Without realising it he gripped the edge of the bed. Everything round him was swaying gently. Things moved slowly as if brushed in a breeze: the curtains, his bedclothes, the nurse. Suddenly, out of nowhere, the ceiling began to rush towards him on his bed! The walls were going to crush him. He was falling.

Terrified, he shouted to the nurse. She was round the bed in a moment and took hold of his hand.

"Don't leave me!" he cried. "What's happening?"

His world continued to press in on him - it was grey and dark - huge objects were swirling round him - his bed wouldn't keep still. He seemed to be pinned to it while the ceiling hovered menacingly over his head. Was he dying, he thought. Was this it?

For several minutes James was trapped in this unreal world. Gradually, however, his surroundings began to recede to their normal proportions and eventually stood still. He began to relax his grip on the nurse. His teeth had been clenched and his eyes tightly shut as everything had hurtled towards him. He began to breathe more easily as the terror subsided. He looked up at the nurse and tried to tell her what had happened.

"Did you feel anything?" he demanded. "What was it?"

Nobody gave an answer as to why this had happened. Neither could anyone give an assurance that it would not happen again. Perhaps it was caused by his drugs, or by the loss of blood he had endured, or perhaps the general trauma and assault upon his body by the accident was leaving more than physical scars. Whatever the reason, James felt shaken by it all. He realised that there was so much outside the doctors' or nurses' or his own control. He thanked God that he at least had things in hand. Everything else was a bit too uncertain to rely on!

It was hard for James to explain his attitude to this incident and to the accident itself. So many people expected him to be blaming God for what had happened: to be asking questions as to why God had allowed it; to be asking if he thought he could go on living. Yet James had no such feelings. Yes, he was suffering fear in many unforeseen ways, he had horrible dreams and unending pain from which there seemed no escape. But he had heard God's own voice. That was enough for him. God had given him that to hold onto. As he began to understand how close he had come to death, how uncanny was his recovery, James felt a deep and enduring gratitude to God. If God for some reason had planned this in his life then he was already giving him the grace to accept it.

James wasn't one for going in for deep introspection on what it would be like 'to be only half a man' as the papers were saying. He was stubbornly determined to live even if medical science couldn't explain his survival or agree on the pace of his recovery. He just wanted to get on with it. Give up on life? Never. The thought wasn't allowed to enter his head.

A skipper in Peterhead had sent James a poem in hospital. The man did not profess to be a Christian but a relation of his had written it and he thought James might appreciate it. "Knowing you were that way inclined, like, James," he had added when he saw him again. (see page 9) It expressed so much of what James was feeling that he kept it close beside him and read it often. It could have been written especially for him.

Being allowed home for his first weekend only three weeks after the accident had been a big boost to James. Hardly able to believe that it was possible, he told Margaret as soon as she came in to see him.

"But James..." she stammered, "what will we do? I don't know how to look after you." Margaret had been given no preparation for this. "The steps outside...the bedroom upstairs."

"I told the surgeon we'd cope with any problems," grinned James. And Margaret had to smile.

"Aye. I've phoned the joiner and he's making a wee ramp for the chair to get me up the steps." Always wanting to be a jump ahead James had arranged it all.

Only then, three weeks after the accident to James did Margaret begin to realise what the long term problems might be for her husband. Initially she had only known relief that he was alive. She had been told to expect the worst and it had been obvious that no one, from their own doctor who had cut him out of the hopper to the entire staff of the Intensive Care ward, had expected him to survive it all. It was wonderful that he had proved them wrong. But she had quickly questioned how he would respond to the amputation: "Not both legs? How will he manage with *both* off?" It seemed impossible.

Yet James had not experienced the same revulsion that Margaret had felt either about the accident or at the eventual sight of his shortened legs. Seeing him for the first time in his wheelchair with the plaster off and his trousers pinned up over the stumps, Margaret had been horrified. He seemed to be sitting on nothing at all! His legs just stopped! Although she had looked at his injuries as he lay in bed this seemed more frightening. "This is my husband," she thought. "What's happened? There's only this little bit of him sitting there."

Ashamed of her own feelings but also strangely embarrassed *for* James, Margaret pleaded with him not to display his abnormality so publicly.

"Can you not get back into bed, James - or cover them somehow?" she had asked. "You just look so...so...oh, it's horrible!" and she had broken down. She seemed to have been crying so much lately. It was so difficult trying to be strong. Seeing the harsh evidence of James' suffering Margaret felt selfish in her inability to be more positive and share more of the burden with him. But what could she do? She felt so sickened by it all, and so helpless. And he was in such dreadful pain. There was nothing she could do except watch him swallow more painkillers and pray from hour to hour that he would get some release from it, however brief.

There were also the children to consider. Fiona was not long in school and Graham was only three. How could she explain to them what had happened to their Daddy?

Margaret had told them the day after it had happened, before they could start asking where James was. She wanted Fiona in particular to understand, in case she heard people talking about it the next day in school. Fiona said nothing. She accepted that 'Daddy had had an accident at the factory' and that she would 'see him as soon as he was a little better'. How much was locked away inside her, and how much would be unleashed when James came home for the weekend, Margaret had no idea.

When he did arrive the children were wonderful. They made no fuss at all and seemed to enjoy the novelty of running to get things for him and were intrigued by his wheelchair. They were also puzzled by his stumps with an innocent and genuine curiosity. It made a refreshing change from the horror Margaret had felt or the gory sensationalism that others sought.

The frequent tears were not the only signs that Margaret remained greatly shocked by the accident. The speed with which their lives had been changed left little time for reflection but it all stayed with her: the premonition of disaster she seemed to have had when she had phoned the factory that night and driven down to the jetty, the horror of being told what had happened, and the fear she had known as she waited for news. They remained as ever-rising memories for a long, long time.

And yet she had been prepared in one small way. Three

weeks before the accident Margaret had been given a book. She and James had met a couple from New Zealand who had turned up at Peterhead Assembly of God church one Sunday. They invited them to their house for a cup of tea. The couple had been very friendly and James always loved a chance to talk of people and places he had known overseas. In the end their new friends had stayed in the area for a few days. When they left they had pressed a gift on the Browns - 'as a token of friendship' they had said. It was a book. The New Zealanders had not read it themselves but had seen it in a bookshop and thought it might be interesting. "Hope you enjoy it," they had called as they left.

They had had no idea how important that book was to prove. For it was called *Joni*, the story of a young American girl who had been dreadfully injured after breaking her neck in a diving accident in 1967. The book told of her suffering and rebellion against God but also of her deepening faith and love for him after the tragedy.

Margaret had read it at once and tried to get James to read it but he was too busy.

"We're going flat out - full dinger - to get the production up," he would say. "I just haven't the time."

When the accident had happened so soon afterwards Margaret felt that this book had been given to her in God's merciful plan so that she would be able to face what was ahead a little more easily. The family were so rarely ill she had had no experience of looking after an invalid. Now at least she knew of someone who had known similar tragedy and had come through. Perhaps James would too. This was the first book that Margaret brought him in hospital and he quickly read it. So encouraging did he find it that in his usual, forthright way he had soon donated copies of it to others: the nurses, the physiotherapist, other patients. It told so clearly how someone in a seemingly hopeless condition could praise God in the midst of suffering - no one would be in any doubt as to where James Brown was getting his strength and will to live from!

On that brief visit home to Peterhead James began to discover just how many people had not only heard of his accident but were praying for him too. He had received hundreds of cards and letters but to actually meet some of the friends who had sent them was a real encouragement to him. He even went down in the car with his brother to the harbour and met some folk he worked with. It felt great to be back - even if it was just for a day or two.

Back amongst the family that weekend there was plenty talk about the accident. Various experts and inspectors had been in to look at the factory and could find no fault with it. They had poked about in the machinery taking it apart and putting it back together again but the mystery of how it had all suddenly come to life had never been solved.

Margaret's brother, Joseph, worked in the plant with James and he was able to tell them all that had been done to try and discover the cause. His had also been the responsibility to clear up the plant-room on the morning after the accident. "It was a horrible sight," he told James. "Like a butcher's shop with bits of flesh and bone all over the machinery. We had to put it all into a big, sealed bag and hand it over to the police in case wee bits of you turned up on some rubbish dump. It would've started a murder inquiry, so they said."

He also had a particularly grim story for his brother-in-law. He was reluctant to tell James but thought that he would hear about it eventually anyway. He might as well hear about it now.

"You know the escape hatch at the top of the vertical screw?" Joseph asked. (This lets the surplus ice out if the system should be in danger of jamming.)

"Aye," said James, a bit wary as to what was coming.

"Well," Joseph looked sick as he remembered, "we set the system running to see if everything was free. Something came flying out and nearly landed on top of me. James, it was your right shoe, and your foot and sock were still inside!"

7

AGAINST THE ODDS

Back at the Aberdeen Royal Infirmary on Monday morning, James felt he was ready to face the days that lay ahead. The short time at home had not been easy: negotiating the wheelchair round the house had been frustrating, sometimes even impossible, and he had had some bother with his stumps. As he had lain in bed at home they had been very itchy and he had scratched them too vigorously. They had bled, all through the bandages and soaked the sheets. The blood wouldn't stop and he and Margaret had been given a real fright. The district nurse had had to come out in the middle of the night to stop the bleeding and apply fresh dressings.

Yet he had been home. Somewhere lurking at the back of his mind had been the unvoiced feeling that perhaps he would never be *normal* again; never be able to be a proper parent; never manage to throw off the weakness that dogged him as a result of all that had happened. Having been at home and treated just like one of the family again he was reassured. He was determined to knuckle down to the various programs of drugs and exercise with more energy than before.

His increased vitality, however, was a sore trial to the nurses! They had to keep a close eye on him or he would be out of bed when he should be resting, entertaining visitors at all times of the day, or turning up his radio so that the whole ward could join in with whatever was being broadcast.

"It's just hymns, nurse," he would explain to the staff nurse. "We're just having our own wee Sunday service. And see, the boys are loving it." Sure enough she would see several beaming faces turned towards her, perhaps more pleased that James was upsetting the strict regime of the ward than to be listening to the hymn singing!

For James' ward was under the tight control of Sister Cruikshank. Well known throughout the hospital, Sister Cruikshank was quite a force to be reckoned with. Having trained in the army she ran her ward like a parade ground and the staff and patients alike were clearly in awe of her. To receive her censure was a serious and nerve-racking business! It was perhaps fear of Sister's reprimand that made James' staff nurse so strict with him.

Yet this staff nurse did seem to take a real dislike to James and had no time for what she considered to be his *misbehaviour*, particularly when he disrupted the ward in this way. It was *not* to be tolerated.

The final straw came one day when this staff nurse found James dressing his own wounds. Some of the nurses found the odd shape of the stumps difficult to bandage and the dressings always seemed to be falling off. James had become quite adept at re-bandaging them himself whenever this happened. One day, however, he dislodged the dressing and he had secretly asked an auxiliary nurse for some disinfectant and some cotton wool! Concentrating on trying to tie himself back together again he had not seen the staff nurse approach.

"What on earth do you think you are doing?" she barked. "No one - but no one in this ward is allowed to doctor themselves. Just what do you think you are in hospital for?"

James knew he was beaten. He also knew when enough was enough and very humbly begged her forgiveness. Even so, the nurse informed James that this would be reported to the 'powers that be'. By this she meant the surgeon and - much worse - Sister Cruikshank! The staff nurse would be vindicated when Sister Cruikshank came and gave the ward's troublemaker one of her dreaded tongue-lashings!

Yet when Sister Cruikshank was informed of James' misdemeanour the expected censure did not come. As she stood sternly at the foot of his bed hearing a list of his *crimes* James was careful to be abjectly apologetic but it was not this that helped him. Indeed such humility was very suspicious! Instead it seemed that Sister Cruikshank caught the twinkle in James' eye which belied his words and her lips twitched as she held in a smile. Somehow James had got under her guard and touched the sense of humour which was usually so successfully hidden beneath her brisk personality. But it was beneath her to show her enjoyment of the situation. Stifling her smile into a tight grimace she assumed her usual officious manner and quickly bustled off, leaving nurses and patients staring after her in surprise. What had happened to the lecture? Was James to get off scot-free?

This seemed to be the case and James soon discovered

that in Sister Cruikshank he had made a useful ally. For her word was law. Ignoring the staff nurse's complaints she chose to indulge James and treated him thereafter like some errant schoolboy. It was if she enjoyed being stood up to now and again.

As soon as people heard of James' injuries they often made mention of Douglas Bader, the pilot who had lost his legs in a flying accident. Although James was never able to meet him he quickly read the Bader story and watched the film made of his life.

One man who had been similarly disabled did visit him in hospital. He was the secretary of B.L.E.S.M.A. - the British Limbless Ex-Serviceman's Association. His wife had read of James' accident in their local newspaper. She had phoned Margaret and chatted to her encouragingly. Then she had suggested that her husband who was also a double amputee might visit if James would like it. James, of course, was delighted to meet him. Physiotherapy was so exhausting and walking on the artificial legs was as painful as ever, yet here was this man with *both* legs off *above* the knee walking towards him with just two sticks!

It was so good to speak to someone whose experiences were similar to his own: to hear that phantom pains really *did* go in time, to see that as the wounds healed over walking *would* get easier, to know that it *was* possible not to live like an invalid for the rest of his life. Although there was a long way to go for James this visit was a great inspiration to him. It would be worth the struggle if only he could begin to live normally again.

While James was in hospital he was always aware from the number of letters and visitors he received that people were praying for him. It was wonderful to know. From all over the world cards and messages were sent. Many in Australia wrote to him assuring him of their prayers. It was exciting. He would be getting the 24-hour treatment with people praying at all times of the day! Some had heard of his accident through friends. Others - sometimes even complete strangers like the couple involved in B.L.E.S.M.A. - contacted him having read of his accident in the various newspapers which covered his story. He heard that even the men at sea had learnt of his accident through their ship-to-shore transmitters. First one boat had heard and then another had been contacted:

"Did you hear about the ice-man? Aye, the boss man - Brown," and so the story had spread. On that first night it had gone right across the North Sea, passed among the fleet and causing quite a sensation.

As he began to regain his strength James became increasingly concerned about the business - and about the future of his job. Although he was the Managing Director of the Ice Company there were a number of other shareholders who had invested capital in the venture. These major shareholders were company directors and James was aware that they were already uneasy about the likelihood of him returning to work. Indeed, during his first week in hospital James' second-in-command, Bruce Forsyth, had been temporarily promoted for an indefinite period to his post. All James' personal effects had been removed from his own office as Bruce moved in and they were sent home in a cardboard box to the house. Margaret had been very upset. It was as if she was being told that although James may have survived, he could be of no earthly use to anyone. He had just been discarded. When the Chairman visited James in hospital and told him of the decision James was confused and angry. It was like his colour blindness - or the allergy at sea. This new defect looked like it was going to prevent him doing his job again. James knew that he was seriously injured but would this mean that he had suddenly become ineffective in the business he had himself begun? They seemed to think that because he now had no legs he was completely useless - unfit for anything. Well, he would have to change their minds. He knew that he was going to get better. He would just have to prove to them that he could go back.

His efforts in the next weeks were increased with this motive in mind. Physiotherapy was agony - and exhausting - but he gritted his teeth and took the few extra steps. His wounds throbbed after each session but he would just have to get used to it. The nights were long but they brought him closer to his discharge when he could get back into harness. For he was a relatively young man - just turned forty - and there was a lot that could still be done to improve business operations. And there was the family to think of. When his substitute fell ill only weeks after taking over his job James redoubled his efforts. He had to get back to work.

James' surgeon was a great help to him in this fight to get better, not least in the encouragement he provided. Seeing

James' delight at being able to go home for a short weekend, it was soon arranged that he could go home each weekend if he wished. If he wished? Nothing would keep James back! Even when the road between Peterhead and Aberdeen was blocked by floodwater on his second trip home Margaret and Joseph battled to get him through. The police were turning everyone back but they waited for a while till the waters went down slightly and they were allowed to try it. Even then the only other vehicles on the road were those abandoned on the verge.

After seven weeks in hospital James was itching to get home for good. The only thing that was keeping him in hospital was the need for physiotherapy which would have to continue for many months. His wounds were healing nicely after some initial hitches and the surgical drains which had been inserted into his stumps had been removed. His walking was going quite well although he moved about mainly in the wheelchair: he still required a lot of support while walking on the 'tin legs'. True to character James wasted little time in approaching Mr Mills. What did he think?

Taking his arm the surgeon asked James to show him what he could do. "Let's get you onto those legs and you can give us a demonstration. Take my arm. We'll just go up the ward a little here. Let's see how far you can go."

The others with the surgeon were unhappy about it: "There's no way he can do it," "He's pushing himself too far too soon," "It's crazy!"

James felt the arm under his own grip him tightly. With his own hand he held the wooden crutch firmly under his other arm. Hoisting himself onto the artificial legs tied to his stumps James set his teeth to go up the ward. The next few minutes were excruciating. Up to that point James had only walked between parallel bars with his arms taking much of his weight. He could feel his body shuddering with the effort. But the hand under his arm was strong and firm and the words in his ear were encouraging. Turning round after several yards to return to his bed James faced the other members of staff on the ward round. They were looking amazed and disbelieving. James took new strength. He would show them.

Back on his bed James appealed to Mr Mills: "I checked with my doctor at home," he said. "He says they could fit in daily physiotherapy at the cottage hospital for me. So...can I go?"

Mr Mills was surprised to hear this. "Is that so? Well, it looks like there's little here to keep you" - he ignored the protests from the others on the ward round - "You're free to go."

Immediately James began to make arrangements. Plans buzzed around in his head. He started on his locker - "Must give the nurses the rest of these chocolates. It's like a sweetie shop in here. And I'll need to get a lift home. I wonder if Joseph can manage to come through. The sooner the better. The ambulance strike just now means there won't be any transport and I'm not waiting here for their convenience!"

Now he had been given the 'all clear' nothing could hold him back. Having been offered the chance of a return to some semblance of normality he was ready to grab that chance with both hands.

Margaret, however, was more apprehensive. She was pleased that his recovery was progressing so fast that this could be considered but she felt so unprepared.

"Already, James? But...but how will we manage? I don't know what to do. The weekends are okay. But this is different, James. This is for good." Questions raced through her mind. It all seemed so soon. And nobody had ever given her any instruction in how to deal with someone as badly injured as James. Nobody had advised them or prepared them for the situations which would arise at home. James had been diagnosed as 100 per cent disabled. It was considered that he was handicapped to the greatest degree. And it wasn't as if he was going to recover. He wouldn't suddenly 'grow legs'. How could they adjust to this without a little time and preparation?

Yet Margaret was never to receive any assistance in preparing her for James' homecoming. Everything was learned by trial and error - mainly by error in those early days!

James, however, had quickly learned to dress himself and soon learned how to hoist himself in and out of the bath. Out of his wheelchair he could drag himself along the floor for a short distance. It would have been pitiful to watch this childlike struggle had James not been so happy to be able to get about at all. Margaret was continually worried that he would damage or reopen his wounds by dragging himself over the carpet like this but James was unconcerned. He was only too aware what pressure his stumps were under when he fastened on his crude artificial limbs during the physiotherapy lessons. As the swelling had begun to go down he wore more and more thick stockings - as many as half a dozen at a time on each stump. These often wrinkled and rubbed at the tender, new skin. In addition, a muscle spasm in his right stump had begun to bother him. It was a horrible, shooting pain like a hot electric shock which convulsed through it if he had been trying to do too much. Whatever painkillers he used nothing seemed to touch this crippling pain.

But physiotherapy and getting onto those artificial legs permanently was the way to improvement and early on his first Monday morning back at home James called at Peterhead's cottage hospital. He was anxious to have the treatment first thing in the morning: he didn't want to be too late getting to the factory. Only seven weeks after his horrendous accident James was determined to get back to work.

A more awkward place to work could not exist than Peterhead Ice Company. Sitting out on a short jetty, it is built on various levels. Narrow passageways, steep metal ladders and high catwalks connect one floor to another. Arriving in his wheelchair on that Monday morning James wondered when he would be able to manoeuvre his way round it again. After greeting his surprised staff he got himself onto his artificial legs, stomped his way into the office and round behind his desk. At least here he could get down to some of the paperwork that had been building up. He sat back in his own office chair and began to feel a bit normal again. With his legs hidden from view and his crutches out of sight on the floor beside him it was almost as if he could imagine that it had never happened.

One look into the plant-room, however, was enough to remind him of his disability. One glance over to the thundering machinery brought it all back. As soon as he was able James knew that he would have to go over to the scene of the accident, get his hands right onto the machinery, even get back inside the hopper if necessary! He must have no reservations about being around it again. It was the only way that he would be able to convince himself, far less anyone else, that he was capable of staying in his job.

Unpleasant realities also had to be faced at home. It was lovely to be back - to be out of the rigid routine and the inactivity of hospital life. Yet at home on a permanent basis his tiredness and weakness became much more obvious. James would watch Margaret helplessly as she got the children up for school, washed the dishes, drove her little mini everywhere and ferried him to and fro. She was doing everything.

"You've even got to put out the rubbish - wash the car - all the things I used to do, Margaret. It's not fair on you. It's not fair."

"I don't mind, James."

"But *I* mind," he would reply. It was all so frustrating. "I couldn't even get after Fiona last night when she had her feet up on the couch. I can't even call them in from the garden. I just have to sit here and let you do it. What sort of

Dad does that make me, Margaret? And you're tired too. It's all making more work for you to do. It's not right. It's just not right!"

There was little that Margaret could say to help him. She could only comfort him.

"Fiona and Graham aren't expecting you to do anything," she assured him. "They don't mind."

"Aye, well. I suppose not. I just used to have such a lot of fun with them, that's all. Remember Blackpool this summer? Going down the seafront every morning with them. All the shows. Swimming in the sea. It just seems...well...How am I going to do that again, Margaret?"

"We'll see," she replied. "Don't worry."

Many of the frustrations at home were caused by James' inability to move freely through the house, particularly upstairs. He was determined to walk in the house as much as possible, however. The wheelchair was awkward - too wide for the doorways and steps were impossible on his own. He *had* to get around on artificial limbs. At least, if he fell at home, he thought, there would be the carpet to land on.

On James' first day out of hospital there had been glorious weather. It was a bright autumn day and James looked out of the window longingly. It was so long since he'd been outside on his own. Finally he decided he would give it a try.

"I'm going outside, Margaret," he called, fastening his limbs more tightly. "I've got to do it sometime. It may as well be now!"

Margaret watched him stumble out to the door with his crutches. She wasn't to help him. He wanted to do this himself. She waited nervously to hear a cry as he fell or needed help. The sound she heard was not what she was waiting for. For James was laughing! She went to the front door to see what he was doing: "What's the joke?"

"It's the steps," laughed James. "I just can't work out which leg goes first. I don't know how to go about it."

Feeling like a pair of clumsy contortionists James and Margaret pushed and pulled, propping his back against the doorjamb and shifting his legs and crutches inch by inch down each of the three steps. It was a major operation and he arrived out of breath on the tarmac. Yet he would not be persuaded that he had done enough.

"All that trouble for nothing?" he gasped, red in the face with the exertion. "I'll just take a few steps down the drive. I did it in hospital. I can do it again now."

Margaret watched him from the door. The drive was wide and sloped down to the road at the bottom of the garden. James set off. Slowly, shakily he propelled himself down the drive. The gate at the end was his goal. Running the length of the drive was a low wall and finally reaching the end of the drive James turned gingerly and leaned heavily against it. He smiled back at Margaret. He had walked about twelve yards with only the crutches for support.

Just then a friend who lived across the road from the Browns appeared in his garden. Looking on from a window he had watched James' progress down to the gate. Calling out to James now, he cried, "Good to see you, Jim. Coming in for a coffee?" Although it had been suggested lightheartedly, James did not need another invitation.

"Just a minute, Bill," he replied and with his crutches tightly held under his arms, James lurched the few more yards across the quiet street to Bill's house. When Margaret called round later he was happily ensconced in his friend's sun-lounge, holding forth on the happenings of the past few weeks.

The stairs inside the house remained a problem for James. During the weekend breaks from hospital they had set up a bed-settee downstairs but he was tired of this. He wanted his own bed. And in the struggle to make life as normal as possible sleeping downstairs became a regular bug-bear. The eighteen or so steps to the upstairs landing soon became the focus of his efforts in the first weeks at home. It was a major task. How could he tackle it? He certainly couldn't negotiate the staircase as he had the front steps. A new strategy was clearly required.

One afternoon when Margaret was out James decided that today he would make an attempt. Graham was with him and James chatted to him as he made his way on his artificial legs to the bottom of the stairs: "We'll surprise your Mum, won't we, Graham? We'll both go up and she'll wonder how we got there!"

Graham was as excited as his father. It was as if they were going on some expedition. They were mountaineers - and a carpeted, bannistered Everest beckoned!

James had decided that he would have to clamber up

backwards without his 'tin legs' or his crutches, just using his stumps and his arms to lever himself up the steps. He sat down, therefore, at the bottom to unfasten the 'legs' and left them standing with his crutches in the hall.

The next half hour was an enormous struggle. Pushing himself upwards on his bottom he negotiated each step. It was difficult to balance and he could not push down with his stumps. It was hot work. Graham thought it was great fun! At the age of three he was an old hand at stairs and considered it hilarious that he was now helping Dad!

Finally James reached the top step. He caught his breath. He had done it! He was upstairs. As quickly as he could he pulled himself into one of the front rooms. Margaret was due back any minute. He and Graham clambered onto a chair by the window. Sure enough, they were just in time to see her arrive back in the car. They waved furiously as she walked to the door and laughed down at her shocked face.

"How did you get up there?" Margaret asked as soon as she got in, half laughing, half scolding. "What'll you do next? You can't be left on your own without getting up to something!"

From then on James slept upstairs. He would leave the limbs at the foot of the stairs and would shuffle up the steps getting quicker each time. Getting down was easier. He just slide all the way down on his bottom. What he saved in socks not having to change them every day, he lost in trousers. Several pairs were ruined, wearing away the seat of them on the floor. The carpet did not fare much better. By the time they moved to a bungalow three years later he had worn the stair carpet right through!

Even as he progressed stage by stage towards greater mobility, James only felt his dependence and inactivity more keenly. Each problem overcome seemed to open up others before him. His impatience provided excellent motivation to achieve whatever he was given to do, yet it was frustrating for him to bear. It was a cruel paradox that as each triumph was gained he was looking ahead to the next hurdle. Therefore, as soon as he had been given the wheelchair, he had wanted out of it; as soon as he could stand, he wanted to walk; as soon as he began to walk, he wanted to drive.

While he had been in hospital James had been visited by a minister who was wheelchair-bound. He had wanted to encourage James and in the course of the conversation he had mentioned to James that he drove himself in his own car using hand controls. He had told James of a kit which could be bought to convert a car to be driven in this way. James, who had always loved driving, was delighted to hear this and had sent away to receive this kit as soon as possible.

Having been at home for three weeks James asked his brother-in-law if he would fit them to Margaret's mini - having first asked Margaret, of course! Since the accident James had been driven by others, usually Margaret. Sometimes the salesman at the factory, Tommy Milne, would transport him to and from work. This was a great source of hilarity to the boys at the plant as Tommy was also an amputee, having lost a leg in an accident years before. Driving an automatic car Tommy would roll up to work with James beside him and they'd lurch into work together

- with only one leg between the two of them!

Yet James was eager to get back behind the wheel:

"I'm tired of being taken everywhere," he complained. "It's great to have everyone so willing - but you know me. I never was a good passenger. I always like to be in the driving seat!"

Joseph quickly fitted the controls. It was quite a simple job. As soon as he was finished James clambered in. He found that he could use his left limb to reach the clutch and the other two pedals were controlled by hand. It was a strange sensation to press down with his left leg and not feel anything but it seemed to work. Soon he was out on the road with Margaret beside him. He even ventured out on his own. His first solo trip was down to the harbour. He would give his friends on the quay quite a scare when they saw him driving past on his own!

8
ON THE MOVE

Although he had been discharged from hospital, James was still required to attend regular clinics in Aberdeen. These were every three or four weeks and Margaret would take him in for these appointments. James had begun to drive short distances in Peterhead but this was much further. In addition, Margaret, more than James himself, was not confident enough to let him drive alone. Even if he drove some of the way, and even as he began to tackle the whole journey himself, Margaret always wanted to be with him.

Together, therefore, they would attend Woolmanhill Hospital and sit and wait while the various consultations took place: the doctors would check the healing process, and physiotherapists would give him several sessions in conjunction with the limb-fitters. They attempted to adjust the clumsy, temporary limbs making them slightly less uncomfortable as his swelling slowly reduced: he was still a long way from being fitted with permanent limbs which would be formed to fit snugly round the final shape of the healed stumps.

There was always a long wait while all this took place and James and Margaret were usually there for most of the day. Other patients had to be seen and every slight adjustment to the limbs had to be made in the 'workroom' before they were tested out on James.

It was not only a boring way to spend a day, it was also frustrating. One product of James' accident which had become increasingly noticeable was that his nerves were badly affected. Although the expected breakdown had never occurred, he often seemed to be on edge and would quickly become agitated over seemingly trivial matters. Situations like the interminable waiting at the clinics and the exhaustion of the intermittent walking sessions left him irritable and fractious. In addition, they usually had to take Graham with them to Aberdeen as they were away for such long periods. Trying to keep an active three year old amused in the confined space of the waiting room for hours on end did not help matters at all!

Occasionally, however, James would visit the ward where he had been a patient latterly and where he had become well known. On his second visit to the clinic he was particularly keen to visit them. Through continual exercises and hours of painful practice James had mastered walking for short distances with just one walking stick. It was a difficult and precarious manoeuvre as he had to fling the limbs forward with the top of his legs and his hips. At the same time he had to transfer his weight from one side to the other. Ungainly and prone to disaster as these movements were James was determined to show off his new skill.

"Wait till they see this, Margaret," he had boasted. "And I'll challenge the Sister to some arm wrestling. She told me to keep my strength up. She'll not believe the muscles I've got now."

Margaret glanced at his thin face. Her husband had lost so much weight since the accident that he was still weak and the pain and weariness were leaving their marks. But, she thought, if he was going to be cheerful, she could be too.

"Don't be too sure of yourself, James," Margaret smiled. "It's more likely you'll land on your rear end like you did last night in the living room! That wouldn't impress them very much. Just you watch they don't try to re-admit you."

This was the ultimate threat. James turned to his wife with a quick glance before he realised that she was joking. But the sudden jerk had nearly toppled him as he turned into the ward. He was still very shaky. A quick recovery was required before anyone saw him.

Balanced again he turned to Margaret, "Just watch me!" he grinned.

Just then a loud shout sounded from the nurses' station: "Well, look who's here! Turning up like a bad penny." Sister Cruikshank's wry grin belied her harsh words. Her hearty tones brought some of the other staff over to see what was happening.

"D'you see this," said James taking a step or two. "Not bad, eh?"

"What are you doing with a walking stick, Brown? We thought you'd have thrown them away by now," Sister replied.

"And here was me thinking how well I was doing," he retorted. "Trust you to bring me back down to earth." James tried to look crestfallen but didn't succeed. Behind the ribaldry he could see that she was pleased with him. He and

Margaret stayed chatting to some of the staff. They were all interested to hear of his progress. After the long day spent at the clinic with frustrating delays and inactivity it was just the tonic he needed.

As they left the ward Margaret reminded James of his threat: "What about the arm wrestling challenge?" she whispered.

"Not likely," James replied. "I wouldn't dare!"

When they got home to Peterhead, however, James thought to himself about Sister's teasing. She had only been joking but he pondered over what she had said about walking without his stick. He had been reading the book *Reach for the Sky* again about the injured war-time pilot, Douglas Bader. James picked it up and turned to the sections which tell of Bader's early attempts to walk after he had lost his legs.

"What a man," thought James. "He didn't even use a stick - refused to."

James looked down at his own artificial legs strapped to his stumps and to the stick leaning beside his chair. The crutches were standing against the wall at the other side of the room. He had progressed quickly enough from crutches to sticks. Could he progress now to using neither? Sister was right. He shouldn't just be patting himself on the back at his recovery so far. He should be getting on.

As far as James was aware Bader held no religious convictions and had no faith. But James knew he had the Lord working with him. "Shouldn't I be able to do just as well as Bader, then," thought James, "or even better?"

Heaving himself up from his chair James took his stick and stomped slowly towards the door and leaned against it. Turning round carefully he caught Margaret's attention as she looked up from her chair.

"Watch this!" he cried. His voice was firm and strong.

"Where...what are you doing?"

"Just watch me. I'm going to cross the room - without this," and he tossed the stick he held aside.

"Now, James, you'll fall," warned Margaret, half rising from her chair.

Before she could move towards him, however, James was away, heading across the width of the room. He took one step and paused, and another. His arms were stretched out, wobbling up and down in the air. He was concentrating hard. Then, with a sudden spurt of energy, he took one, two, three, four, five steps before his hands reached out to the wall ahead of him! He took hold of the curtain beside him for support.

"I did it! I did it!" he cried.

Margaret was beside him, hugging him, helping him to a chair.

"I *can* walk. I can *do* it."

Excitement took the edge off the pain yet it was very intense. His full weight had been pressed down repeatedly on his stumps with the impact caused by each step. As he threw himself into an armchair his legs were throbbing - but he didn't care. He wouldn't think of it. He had walked. That was what mattered. Just when he had been fed up and irritated by the restrictions of the day, God had provided the incentives. God was in charge - directing what was going on. "He really knows me inside-out," James marvelled. Just when his energy had been sapped by all the day's protracted exertions he had been encouraged to attempt what many considered to be impossible. Well, he was learning to 'tune out' pain, ignoring it by focusing on other things. This present happiness and relief was as good a focus as any.

At his next physiotherapy session James was keen to surprise the staff with this new ability. Using his crutches to take him along the corridor to the treatment room, he slung them casually over his shoulder before opening the door and walking in - unaided. Just to see their shocked faces made the effort worthwhile.

Yet as he was attempting more and more James was finding that it needed every ounce of his energy and concentration to keep going. Working at the factory each day was particularly difficult as he had to give maximum effort both to getting himself there in the morning and then to carrying out his normal job once he arrived. This strain combined with the fragile state of his nerves made life at home sometimes fraught with tensions.

Coming in from work James would be tightly wound up and needed quietness and peace to help him relax. Margaret would try to give him the time to rest like this but with two young children in the house it was never easy. Fiona and Graham were too young to understand. They would run boisterously round the house and the garden or be in and out of every room. James would become irritable and then be frustrated with being so highly strung which only intensified the problem.

Lunch times were particularly difficult. James always came home for his lunch and he would be wrapped up in whatever he had been doing that morning. Having to concentrate so hard on what was at the forefront of his mind he found it impossible to relax. Fiona and Graham were always there for lunch too: Fiona came home from school and Graham was in the house with Margaret anyway. Like any children they would chatter together and would be full of activity. Perhaps aware of the tensions they would misbehave and annoy one another. Then at the table they would nudge and poke each other till there was rarely a moment's peace. James was unable to cope. Wanting to keep under control so as not to upset the children he only became more agitated. Something had to be done before they all suffered.

After one particularly fraught meal time Margaret and James received a visit from their local Health Visitor who called occasionally to check up on James. Although primarily concerned with his physical well-being she was sympathetic when Margaret explained their current problem to her.

Help was at hand and the Health Visitor arranged for Graham to attend one of the few nursery schools in Peterhead. He would be looked after for a few hours each day, including lunch times, so the house would be quiet for James when he needed it. Fiona would be able to have her mid-day meal at school.

Margaret felt lost for a while without her little boy beside her all day. She felt terrible pangs of guilt for leaving him with others when he was so young. He was really such a placid, gentle boy. It was a shame that he should have to suffer for something which was not his fault. But as James' nerves began to improve it seemed worthwhile - and Graham was enjoying himself too.

It had been a simple practical solution and it was much appreciated. It also meant that Graham no longer had to sit through weary clinic appointments and James' physiotherapy sessions. She could now leave him in capable hands.

One place where James found he could relax was in the water. Having heard of some amputees who were excellent swimmers James was keen to try. He had to wait until dressings were no longer required on his stumps but as soon as he could he wanted to make an attempt to swim. A friend of his, Ronnie Glennie, was the janitor at the local special school for disabled children and Ronnie had mentioned that it had a small and easily accessible pool.

"I'd love to see if I can still swim," James asked. "I used to love it."

"Well, I'm sure we can arrange it," Ronnie replied. "Why not come down some night and you can have the place to yourself. I'll give you a hand."

"Great. I'm dying to give it a go."

Although he needed help to get to the school and to get ready the cubicles were specially designed to accommodate wheelchairs and James just detached his limbs and wheeled himself out of the changing rooms and out to the water's edge. He was very nervous as he looked down at the water.

Would he be able to float? He wouldn't be able to touch the bottom. How would he push off from the side? More importantly, how would he get in?

This last question was soon answered as Ronnie helped him out of his chair and positioned him on the top step. These sloped into the pool and James slowly used his hands to lower himself from one step to another until he was in the water. Then with Ronnie beside him he pushed off from the side with his hands and found himself - floating!

"Eee - I can float," he cried, his voice echoing across the water. "This is great!"

Using his arms James pulled himself through the water. It was easy - the easiest movement he'd been able to make since the accident. The lightness of his legs made him very buoyant and his arms had been strengthened by all the exercises which he still had to do. He found that he could even use his stumps to propel himself. He felt so free and mobile - and normal, for a change. Here there were no clumsy, abrasive limbs to slow him down, no pain or weakness to hold him back.

Although the pool was small James swam round and round, managing to swallow great mouthfuls of water as he shouted his delight to his friend.

Soon James was regularly visiting the pool in the local community centre where there was more scope. He even joined the local sub-aqua diving club, delighted that he could pick up an old hobby from his Australian days. Fiona and Graham often went with him to the pool, undaunted by the sight of their father struggling to the pool-side with his stumps in full view of everyone. Margaret was unable to be so nonchalant. For a long time she was unable to watch him do this and remained embarrassed and sickened by it. She could not pretend to have James' lack of concern. For it was not just at the local pool he would do this. Even by the sea on holiday he would drag himself along a crowded beach to reach the water. Margaret would be left to watch the horrified stares which followed him into the water yet for James it was worth the struggle and the unpleasant attention just to be able to swim again. So proficient did he become that he entered the Handicapped Games in 1981 held in Bishopbriggs and came away with two gold medals and one silver!

The freedom James found in the water was unfortunately never possible on dry land and James continued to have difficulties, particularly in the factory. Even as he tried to resume his duties he was constantly reminded of his handicap. He became accustomed to falling on the hazardous factory floor where a mere drop of oil or water, or a brief lapse in concentration on James' part could have him tumbling to the ground where he lay in a helpless heap. From this position it was extremely difficult to get up. He would feel like a man on skis for the first time - as soon as he would find a grip with one limb the other would slide away from him! Once when this happened the plant was deserted and he floundered about on the floor on his own getting more and more frustrated. His trousers became tattered and coated in the oil on which he had slipped. Eventually he had to drag himself across the plant room floor to where a great coil of rope was hanging. Only by pinning his body against the wall and then pulling himself up this rope by the strength in his arms, did he manage to get upright again.

Part of James' job as Managing Director of the Peterhead Ice Company had always been to communicate with the Scandinavian suppliers of the factory's machinery. When it was decided that a visit would have to be made to Sweden in connection with this James would have been the obvious choice to go. Indeed, it was difficult to see who else could be responsible for this. But the trip would mean a lot of travelling, meetings in Stockholm and elsewhere and visiting various factories throughout Sweden. When it was arranged for less than a year after James' accident he and Margaret became concerned. How could this long and tiring trip be achieved? They were only too aware how precarious was his walking in an unknown place, how helpless he could become when he was unable to keep his balance. It was possible to negotiate a short distance on the streets of Peterhead where willing assistance was usually available. It was another thing to contend with a jostling airport crowd or the traffic of a congested city centre.

Yet as the time drew near for James to go, all their misgivings were gradually dismissed. Not only would the company secretary - a local lawyer and a good friend of James'- travel with him, but all the necessary facilities would be provided: wheelchairs would carry him around the huge airports, fork-lift trucks would lift him in and out of the planes, and hotels with lifts would be booked near the various airports. All the arrangements were carefully made. It seemed to be possible after all. If that was so, James was prepared to enjoy himself!

When the trip eventually came, however, it was beset with disasters. Although they thought that all the travel arrangements had been made, James' handicap was a source of continual problems. The combination of trains, aeroplanes, city tube lines and ferries held unforeseen difficulties if anything beyond the planned arrangements was attempted. This lack of freedom seemed to underline James' disability again and again.

Even from the start James and his friend Colin had problems. On arriving at Heathrow airport from Aberdeen, James and Colin booked into an airport hotel. It was evening and their flight to Stockholm was not due to leave until the next morning. Keen to behave as normally as possible and unwilling to miss the chance to see some of the capital at night, James suggested that they take the tube into London and go for their evening meal. If he was unable to negotiate the escalators in the tube stations James was assured that a wheelchair could be found.

The journey into the city went smoothly. Able to find a seat both on the platform and then on the tube itself he was able to walk to the exit. Having caught a taxi outside they quickly found a restaurant and settled down to their meal. This travelling business is easy, thought James. No problem!

Returning to their hotel at Heathrow, however, was another matter. By the time their meal was over and they were ready to leave it was getting late and James was both tired and sore. The exertions of this first day were beginning to tell. The last thing he wanted was the long journey back to the airport. It had to be done nevertheless, so they hailed a taxi not far from the restaurant and managed to catch a Heathrow-bound tube. The city stations were still busy and help was close at hand.

But the situation was different when they arrived at Heathrow. It was nearly midnight and the platform was deserted. Nobody else left the train. No guards or staff were to be seen. Where could they get a wheelchair? James was in no state to walk anywhere - far less up flights of steps. Looking up at the steps and ramps which led to the surface, James knew that he would never make it to the top.

"You go on, Colin," he reasoned. "Perhaps you'll find someone as you go up."

Ignoring him, Colin was looking around for ideas. He couldn't leave his friend, a disabled and now virtually immobile man, stranded in a deserted city station. What could he do? Suddenly he spied the solution. Before James knew what was happening Colin had grabbed a luggage trolley and thrust him bodily inside.

"Hey, watch it!" cried James as Colin set off at a run, pushing the trolley up the first ramp. Yet the relief to be off his legs was wonderful and he did not complain for long. Indeed, he began to enjoy himself. At least there was no one to witness his ungainly, not to say undignified mode of transport!

Reaching the top Colin was exhausted. He leant against the trolley while James hoisted himself out. Landing again on his legs was excruciating. He wondered how much more he could take. His stumps felt very swollen.

"Right then - a taxi," said Colin. "Take a seat here, James. You're not fit to take another step." He pointed to a bench on the pavement and helped James to it before setting off to find some transport that would take them on their final stage back to the hotel. Although it was barely half a mile away - indeed they could see it clearly from the tube station - there was no way that James could walk. And another excursion in the luggage trolley was out of the question!

Colin was gone for what seemed a long time. James began to get cold and was longing for his bed - just to lie down. His stumps were throbbing so much that he doubted he would sleep.

Finally Colin returned in a taxi. It seemed that the driver had initially refused to go such a short distance. He must have thought that this Scotsman wandering around Heathrow after midnight and wanting a taxi to take him a few hundred yards must be somewhat under the influence! When the driver had realised the reason for the unusual request he was extremely apologetic and couldn't do enough to assist the weary James into the taxi. He was very interested and plied James with questions on the brief trip to the hotel. Almost too tired to reply James was grateful to finally get to his hotel room and fall back onto his bed. He unstrapped the vice-like limbs and let them fall to the floor. He hardly dared touch the tender stumps. He was exhausted. What a night! What a start to their trip!

The flight to Stockholm and the various meetings and subsequent visits to factories along the Swedish coast went smoothly with all the arrangements having been made for James' convenience. Cars and wheelchairs were always on hand and he was even able to negotiate the Swedish trains with some assistance. It was good for James to be able to participate as fully as he had always done before.

It was when they reached Helsingborg in the south at the end of the trip that further problems arose. The business having been transacted, all that remained of the journey was to cross by ferry to Denmark and then fly home from nearby Copenhagen. But James was in no hurry to board the ferry. He still had some shopping to do.

"It won't take long, Colin," he explained. "I've just to get some wee presents for the kids. I always take something back from these trips - and this one's special, like." James grinned. "Every other time I've had my own legs with me!"

"Aye, well, if we're quick..." answered Colin. "And you're not too tired are you?"

Shrugging off this idea James had headed off to the shops with Colin in tow and was soon laden with bags.

"D'you think I've gone a bit over the top?" James asked.

"Never mind," exclaimed Colin. "Have you seen the time? We'll have to make a dash for it!"

"You're kidding? We'll get a taxi to the harbour, no bother."

But the centre of Helsingborg was very busy and no taxis seemed to be for hire. It became obvious that James and Colin would have to walk to the ferry terminal - and quickly! Although it was little more than a quarter of a mile across town the roads were extremely hazardous for James. Broad, busy streets were crisscrossed by tramlines making James stumble in the jostling crowd. To make matters worse it began to pour with rain and James and Colin were soon soaked. The pavements became slippery underfoot and even more treacherous. James was soon in difficulties. The walking he had done during the day and the shopping expedition had tired him already. Soon he was hobbling along with one arm on Colin's shoulder and the other clutching his parcels as well as his stick. Colin urged him on. Time was ticking away yet as he tried to rush James could feel the skin on his stumps being rubbed away with the friction and pressure caused by the limbs.

Finally, however, they reached the harbour and found their boat quite easily. Stumbling in with Colin bearing almost all his weight and soaked by the torrential rain, James felt very conspicuous as well as sore. Throwing themselves onto their seats, Colin turned his flushed face to James.

"Are you okay?" he asked. Having been reassured that James was all right, Colin was prepared to be annoyed - "You and your shopping!" But looking at their wet clothes and dripping hair he seemed to see the funny side of it and began to laugh.

"Remind me," he chuckled, "never to travel with you again!"

Having travelled once, disasters and all, James was reassured that at least it was possible and quickly finalised his plans to take the family on holiday. They had been unable to have a proper summer holiday because of his health. James now wanted to give them all a treat. As soon as he could he booked a few weeks in Florida.

The subsequent holiday was great fun although it made them realise what considerations had to be made for James. Not only did they have to rely on the airport staff (James had no desire to repeat the Heathrow luggage trolley experience!), but they also had to think about their accommodation. Was it accessible? Were there any ramps instead of steps for a wheelchair? Would they have to walk to the beach? Although it was not ideal they were able to relax and enjoy themselves. James' biggest thrill was being able to hire a hand controlled American car and drive the family wherever they wished.

Yet, whatever he achieved both at work and in his own time, James still found that he continually had to prove himself in his job. During the months after the accident he had concentrated his efforts on improving the profitability of the company. James was confident that an increase in profits would convince the Board of Directors as nothing else would that he was not a hindrance but an asset. Having taken a course in business studies prior to his accident he felt able to cope with the financial and managerial aspects of his job more efficiently than ever before. To his satisfaction profits increased and targets were quickly reached throughout the year. Although he was unable to devote as many extra hours to the factory as he had done previously, business was continuing to improve. James was convinced that God was honouring his trust in him and it was thrilling to see. By the time of his first salary review since his accident James was satisfied with the results he could produce: not only was the factory maintaining production, he had increased its profitability by twenty per cent.

But James was in for a nasty shock. When the time came for James' salary to be considered accusations rather than congratulations were forthcoming.

"Brown doesn't do anything but sit behind a desk." "We can't have a Managing Director who doesn't get his hands dirty."

Even the industrial injuries benefit and mobility allowance to which James was entitled were mentioned. It seemed as if James was to receive a reduction in his pay rather than an increase!

James was offended particularly because so much of his effort had been focused on becoming more agile round the ice plant. He recalled his early ascent to the highest point in the factory where he was aware that the men were beginning to gather regularly for a sly cup of tea, out of his reach. Crawling and clambering up the succession of spiralling ladders and steep stairways one day, James had come upon the men suddenly. The surprise on their faces had made him laugh.

"You thought you were safe up here, eh?" he had challenged them. "Well - I've caught you!" (It would have spoiled the entertaining effect if he had told the men that the tortuous climb had taken him over half an hour, he had ruined a good pair of trousers and he could have screamed with the pain.)

Now it seemed that all this was not enough. The fact that the Board seemed to have no sympathy with him James took as a sort of backhanded compliment, but he was unprepared for this seemingly unjust and harsh treatment over his pay. Thankfully other directors agreed with him and after a battle of words James received the salary increase to which he was entitled.

Relations with some members of the Board of Directors were not improved by James' claim for compensation. Soon after the accident James had been advised to consult a solicitor and to register a claim against the company and their insurers. This had been done but it was proving to be a very difficult case. The experts who investigated the scene of the accident had been unable to determine its cause: it remained a mystery. The company, therefore, were unwilling to admit liability and James could understand and appreciate this. In addition, James had no wish to accuse any employee of his or to put the responsibility for his accident at anyone's door. Indeed, as he was Managing Director, if any fault had been found he may have been blamed for it ultimately anyway!

James' solicitor was faced, therefore, with a problematic case. What added to the difficulties were James' rapid improvements and his obvious delight in all that he was still able to achieve. When asked to explain what he was now unable to do James was too full of what he *could* do to be preoccupied with any failures.

"I suppose I'll not be water-skiing or jogging again," he would laugh. Such enthusiasm did not help his case!

In the end the case dragged on for five years. A claim had been made for £75,000 on the grounds of pain, suffering and trauma, and on the fact that with no guarantee of employment

James could find himself in a limited labour market. But this claim was contested. Delays and prolonged legal proceedings ensued. Yet as the final hearing approached after the five years, James took an unusual decision. Rather than take the claim any further he agreed to settle out of court. He had no wish to stand in the witness box and be responsible for accusing his friends and colleagues of causing this freak accident. In addition, there was no guarantee of success. In the end he received only a fraction of what he had claimed - barely a tenth.

Yet what was money? He could do without the compensation claim. What was at the forefront of all their minds at this time was much more important, much harder to bear. For James had other reasons for not wishing to appear in court. Only months previously both James and Margaret had been placed in the witness box and cross-examined under different but much more traumatic circumstances. James had no desire to be reminded of the pain and grief of that time. It was debilitating for him in ways that the loss of his legs had never been. For James had lost much more than his health and his mobility. In this second, much more tragic accident, just four years after his own, he had lost his only son.

9
GRAHAM

It was a bright Sunday afternoon. Spring was just slipping into summer and as James drove along the road towards Peterhead, the May sunshine speckled and shimmered over the fields along the roadside. Young grass swayed in the breeze drifting in off the sea.

In the back seat Fiona was sitting looking out of the window while Graham was curled up in sleep. He often seemed to doze off during a journey, however short. For a change Fiona was sitting behind her mother - James could see her daydreaming as he looked in the mirror - and Graham was behind his father. When they had both piled into the car Fiona had slid into the back seat and taken Graham's usual place.

"That's where Graham sits," Margaret had corrected her but she had been determined to stay where she was. Graham had gone round to the other side without a fuss.

This Sunday afternoon had been like any other for the Browns. It was part of the regular family routine that each Lord's Day after lunch James and Margaret would head off in the car with the children to visit Margaret's parents in nearby Cairnbulg. There they would spend the afternoon before heading back to Peterhead for a quick snack and then church at night. Returning after this visit the children were often tired and James would enjoy the peaceful drive, chatting now and again to Margaret beside him. Passing through the little village of Crimond the road was very quiet - a lovely day.

As they turned into a clear stretch of road James saw that the one car ahead of him was beginning to break as the driver indicated that he was turning right. James decelerated behind him. Just then James suddenly noticed a car appear over the horizon, screaming towards them on the opposite side of the road. It seemed to be travelling incredibly quickly. It would be upon them in a moment.

"Look at the speed of that car," James exclaimed to Margaret. "It's going to cause an accident..."

The words were hardly out of his mouth when the driver of the speeding car, a powerful Capri, must have seen the car ahead of James beginning to turn right. He tried to swerve. Brakes shrieked. Almost upon them the Capri was travelling too quickly to complete such a sudden manoeuvre. James and Margaret sat mesmerised - seconds dragged - as the car screeched wildly out of control. Tyres wailed painfully as it spun across the road. Missing the car ahead of James, but with a terrible inevitability, the Capri smashed violently into the fence at the side of the road!

But it wasn't over. As Margaret and James watched helplessly, now almost stationary behind the first car, the Capri bounced as if made of rubber back into the road. It ricocheted across the tarmac. It was heading for them! It couldn't miss! With an unstoppable force the car slammed, broadside on, into them! They were hit!

Momentum propelled the two cars sideways off the road and carried them into a nearby field. Coming to rest on the grass James could see the crumpled Capri somersaulting ahead of them before it too finally rocked - then shuddered - then stopped.

Everything was still. Nothing moved.

Having caught his breath James turned to his door and tried to pull the handle. Nothing happened. It was stuck. The door bulged inwards where they had been hit. Turning to Margaret he could see her looking at him, too scared to ask how he was.

"I'm okay," he assured her. "You?" Nodding quickly she began to fumble with her door. It was undamaged. She clambered out. Fiona behind her was shakily doing the same.

"My new hat," Fiona was wailing in a shocked sort of voice. It was squashed and dented and she pointed to it in the seat she had just left.

"I'm stuck, Margaret," James called. "The door's jammed." He could feel panic creeping over him. This trapped sensation was the feeling he hated. He struggled feverishly with the door.

But Margaret wasn't listening. Looking into the back seat where Fiona was pointing at her damaged hat she could see Graham slumped forward in his seat. Assuming that he was still asleep she leaned into the car from Fiona's side and shook him.

"Come on, Graham. Time to wake up - we've had an accident."

He didn't respond. Instead his head lolled lifelessly back against Margaret's hand. With one look she understood. Letting go, she sat back on her heels and looked down at the little crouching body. There was a quiet pause. Then, "He's dead..."

James was still struggling to get free.

"No, no. I can't believe it..." he gasped. He had just completed a first aid course a few months previously. If he could just get free, he could save him.

"He's gone," Margaret repeated. James managed to twist himself round in his seat until he could see his son. Realisation dawned as he too saw Graham's face. He understood at once what had happened. Graham had been flung across the car with the force of the impact and had hit Fiona's window. Just by looking at the terrible injuries to Graham's face and head it was obvious that he would have been killed instantaneously. He would have been dead even before the recoil put him back in his own seat.

Turning back slowly to face the front, James sat very still. He no longer struggled to be free. He was numb. He just leaned back against the head rest and waited to be released.

Other cars began to stop to help and soon an ambulance arrived. James was finally released from the car and virtually carried across the grass. He and Margaret sat with Fiona in the ambulance. Nobody seemed to be badly hurt and they watched while the police, ambulance men, passing motorists and the other drivers wandered around. James recognised the driver of the Capri as a young man from Peterhead. He was only twenty one and James knew his father quite well.

But the young man said very little to them. James wondered if he realised what he had done. Even as he thought of it James began to shake. He felt crushed by it all - as if all the air had been knocked out of him. It was all so final. The questions of the police and the doctors seemed so irrelevant and he couldn't even think about the answers. As the ambulance drove them away from the scene through to Peterhead James could think of nothing but that they were leaving Graham behind. Only six years old he had never been apart from the family before. So painful was this first wrench that James could think of nothing else.

Yet Margaret seemed to be so strong and calm. In the days that followed, filled with preparations for the funeral, giving statements to the police, attending to those who called to give their condolences, she remained controlled and restrained. Although she would not talk of it much it seemed as if she had come to terms with it at once.

James, in contrast, could talk about little else. It seemed to come pouring out of him, his words immersed in tears and useless 'if onlys'. Always a man of immediate reactions his grief was violent and exhausting. The sense of loss and emptiness was only intensified for him by the succession of petty arrangements that had to be made. Most harrowing of all was the identification of Graham's battered body in the mortuary.

"Aye. That's him," was all James could say as he looked through the glass panel before quickly turning away. Barely recognisable, the sight of the still, straight body only underlined the finality of the tragedy. Graham was not there.

He had gone. It was over.

But intense feelings such as these could not be sustained and as the days passed James found ways of adjusting to Graham's death. He could not go on knowing such powerful grief. As if to defend his weary emotions James began to switch off his mind to the pain. As he had done after his own accident he forced himself to think of other things. He must blot it out and live as if it had never happened. Soon he was almost telling himself that it had happened to someone else, to another family. Shielding himself behind this pretence, and therefore externalising it all, he felt able to cope. He could speak then quite factually, even graphically about the accident as long as it was distanced from him in this way. As the inevitable court case loomed and statements were taken he felt able to respond calmly and coherently to the lists of questions.

But James' and Margaret's reactions did not coincide. Just as he was beginning to remove himself from the tragedy and to hide behind this cloak of pretence, Margaret's grief began to unfold. Held together by the necessary events and procedures of the funeral, and possibly contained by the sudden shock of it all, only afterwards did the loss take its effect. Then, after the seemingly quiet acceptance, the pain was unleashed. Between tears and confused anger Margaret longed to talk to James. She needed to share her grief with him and spoke of Graham often, recalling the painful events of that Sunday afternoon. She seemed to get some relief from talking. It seemed to help.

But James felt torn apart by these memories. Reciting

them to others - policemen, solicitors, even relations - was bearable: he could force himself to be removed from it. But with Margaret there could be no such pretence. His only defence from the pain was stripped away. It was *their* son they were talking about, nobody else's. Seeing Margaret so upset and voicing questions that he hadn't dared to let himself ask, he felt torn and pulled apart inside. He couldn't speak. He couldn't respond. The closeness of their relationship paradoxically seemed to cripple their joint recovery: seeing such intense pain in each other made it so much harder to bear.

During those days Margaret was demanding answers which James could not give:

"Why Graham?" "Why not one of us?" "Why should he be taken from us?" "What harm had he ever done to anyone?"

James could give no explanations. "You know that there are no answers, Margaret," he would reply. "Not on this side of time."

Although they both knew that there were no simple solutions to be found, this knowledge could not quell the questions. The meaning behind it all remained obscured to them. They could never understand. What made it perhaps more difficult was that they knew that understanding was not required of them in God's eyes. He only wanted faith. James and Margaret prayed continually that this would be given to them so that it might become a little easier from day to day.

For Graham had been such a generous, kind-spirited boy. 'A Mammy's boy' they had called him and Margaret often recalled particular incidents where he had shown his simple kindness. Through tears and not comprehending James' reluctance to hear, she shared memories like that of the school sports where he had won three races, receiving three ribbon 'medals'. When Margaret had seen him later wearing only two she had asked him about the third.

"Oh, aye," he had replied with unconscious selflessness. "But Drew didn't win any so I gave him one of mine." Acutely responsive to other's unhappiness even at the tender age of six, it all seemed even more unfair that he should be taken.

As time passed they looked together once more at old family videos in which Graham was always present. Together Fiona and her parents sat in the living room and watched the screen as she and Graham played together, opened Christmas presents together and pulled faces for the camera. Although only ten, Fiona also responded to his special kindness. On one occasion James had filmed them having a snowball fight in the garden. Fiona saw that it was characteristic of Graham that he became upset when he inadvertently hurt her. Sorrowful and comforting he had told her that she could throw one back at him if she wanted to. Watching these scenes many months afterwards, tears were never far away.

Yet Fiona spoke only rarely about her brother after his death. Gravely shocked by the two accidents that had hit the family and a witness to the tragic suddenness of the latter, she seemed to retreat into herself. Where she and Graham had spent hours together in her room chatting and playing,

Fiona now sat alone. Solitude now seemed natural and she only permitted her imagination and feelings free rein in the writing of elaborate stories and poems for herself. This fabricated world was her own to control and create. In it she seemed to escape. Here she could find a response to the cruelty, first of her father's near escape from death and then of the loss of her little brother.

Time is often considered to be the great healer, yet for the first months after Graham's death it seemed as if they were not being allowed to recover. Just when it seemed that it was becoming easier, incidents - even little things - would awaken the feelings. The smallest events seemed capable of arousing the strongest grief. They began to feel that grief was holding them with some relentless grip. It just would not let them go but penetrated so many of their activities and became interwoven in their daily lives.

The first of these incidents was simply the arrival of a photograph. Only two weeks before the accident the family had gone to the local photographer to have passport shots taken in preparation for a holiday. While they were there James had insisted that they should have a group photograph taken as a family.

"But we're not dressed for it," Margaret had claimed. "Another time, James."

But he had been adamant. "No. We don't have one of us all together." So the photograph had been taken.

Now, only weeks after the family had been so suddenly depleted, this photograph arrived. Although they were grateful for this memory eventually, at the time it was like the twist of a knife in their wounds - too vivid a reminder of what had been.

Even the holiday for which the passport photographs had been taken brought its own difficulties. Tickets had already been bought, reservations had been completed. Now it all had to be rearranged. Delays were required although they were advised by friends and relations still to take the holiday. Yet they were three now instead of four. Many explanatory phone calls had to be made and the circumstances had to be described again and again. Even when they eventually took the holiday they were stopped at the immigration desk: Where was the son who appeared on James' passport but was no longer with them? For some reason it was these little things, the details, which had the greatest capacity to rekindle the most powerful feelings. Perhaps it was simply because they were unprepared for them that they were able to continually stir the ongoing pain with such force.

The worst of these times was undoubtedly during the trial of the young driver who had caused the accident. Although they had tried to prepare for this, it was very traumatic for them. Asked to appear in court and cross-examined in the witness box, Margaret and James relived the horror of the experience again and again. Coming as it did at the height of Margaret's grief, James wanted to be able to support her more, feeling acutely his own muddled inadequacy: although he could protect himself by mentally removing himself from the immediacy of it, he could not do the same for his wife.

He turned again and again to vehement prayer and claimed God's strength. He knew that this brutal reminder could be the final straw in a succession of traumatic events which had invaded their lives in recent years. Here again, with Graham's death, their lives had been cut into and rearranged - this time most cruelly of all. Yet to blame God for it would, James knew, be futile. Just as he couldn't blame God for the loss of his legs so he couldn't blame him for Graham's death. They were there, the innocent party in a crash, caused by a young driver going too fast. Perhaps that was what made it more difficult - a more bitter pill to swallow. For in this accident, unlike his own, there was someone to blame. There was a person who was responsible for it. When the final sentence was pronounced on the young driver it was incredibly lenient: a short driving ban and a fine of three hundred pounds. James was disgusted. This could not be reconciled with the pain that they were suffering.

Margaret's predicament was particularly difficult as she and Graham had been particularly close. Being so young he had spent much of his time with her. James understood that her grief as a mother was especially sore. He also felt that her suffering after his own accident had been more acute than his own in many ways: she was the one who had been forced to look on and watch his struggles and had given more thought to the consequences. While James had been so busy recovering, Margaret had borne all the pain at second hand. It would have been easy for her to brood over it all then - it would be easy to brood now.

But just as time had allowed the acuteness of that pain

to decrease, so, with time, did the grief over Graham become less immediate. It could never be removed but it was not so keenly felt. Gradually normal life had to begin again. James had the factory and he became immersed in it as soon as possible. Much later, as much as a year afterwards, Margaret opened a shop in town renting out Christian videos. These videos were a long-time hobby of James' and he was always adding to his large collection. Although her heart was not really in it, Margaret agreed to it. For what she needed most of all was a new routine. So much of each day before Graham's death had been wrapped up in him: taking him to and from school, playing with him, feeding him, and usually a few of his friends as well, going over his reading with him or whatever piece of homework he had in the evening, and then packing him off to bed. Afterwards it was easy to feel that these parts of the day were empty. Watching his friends run off to school or play near the house did not help. The shop, they felt, might fill these hours so that memories would not have too strong a hold. They must take second place. This would be a sign, therefore, that life was beginning again. It was something new - a fresh start.

10

THE MAN FOR THE JOB

James' mobility was greatly increased when he received his first 'suction legs'. These were his first artificial limbs he was given which truly resembled human legs. The rigid 'pylons' as the first limbs were called had been thrown away and the interim limbs were returned. Now these new, definitive limbs could be fitted.

These new limbs also gave James much more confidence, not to mention comfort. The right one even had a knee made of soft, spongy material which moved as he walked. It also had an ingenious locking mechanism which he could activate to help him stand unaided without it giving way. Best of all, the suction gripping system dispensed with all the straps and buckles which had secured the first limbs. Instead these clung like limpets to his stumps. Light and flexible and with the moving knee joint, they allowed James to walk further than before without tiring so easily. Scores of adjustments, new mouldings and sophisticated improvements later, it is these suction limbs, perhaps the best artificial legs available, that James wears to this day.

Yet there are difficulties attached to them, not least the fact that James has to strictly control his weight in order to fit into them. Putting on even a few extra pounds can mean that the sockets will no longer fit over his stumps. (Christmas time can be particularly dangerous: it gives a new perspective to overeating that he might eat so much he might no longer be able to walk!) As soon as he had discovered his ability to swim again James used this exercise to keep his weight down. Sometimes he swims as many as forty lengths of the pool at a time, battling to keep off the inches.

The new limbs not only allowed James to be more mobile, however, they also improved the appearance and style of his walking gait. Although on one level this change was simply cosmetic, this improvement was an important one. Now James could *look* as 'normal' as he clearly felt. The early metal pylons with their robotic appearance and clumsy, clanking movements had often attracted the attention which James always preferred to avoid. Even the later limbs had forced him to walk very stiffly and the complex straps had been quite restrictive. Now those who do not know of his injuries barely notice anything unusual, even when he is on his feet. Sitting down he looks as normal as anyone else.

Yet this air of normality is deceptive, for no improvements can change the physical facts. Even as James does more and more - drives his own car, swims and scuba dives, holds down a responsible job and enjoys numerous other interests - these achievements will always require extra effort, extra determination. He must always give more of himself than those for whom these are simple tasks. For the rest of his life therefore, the activities which an able bodied man would consider to be every day events, James will always find difficult and a struggle. Although he achieves a semblance of normality, he is invariably achieving much more. In addition, by attempting and excelling at normal activities he inadvertently sets himself apart: by overcoming so much he becomes *more* than normal. This is the cruel irony, that by trying so hard to fit in, rising above pain and battling with fatigue, he will always be remarkable, always be different - yet these are the very attributes he is striving to avoid.

Perhaps because his disability is no longer particularly obvious - he is not bed-ridden or wheelchair-bound - more is often expected of James than one might expect. At the same time James has come to expect more of himself - sometimes even forgetting that he is disabled! This has many positive outcomes, particularly when James is able to sense that his work or achievements are valued for their own sake and he is able to make people forget that he is a victim of what happened one night in a factory some years ago. Indeed, in the face of his enthusiasm it would be hard to maintain any feelings of pity or horror for long.

But another product of this forgetfulness is also frustration and disappointment when his disability still intrudes upon his life. Acceptance of his injuries occurred early on, but acceptance of the continual inconveniences still have to be regularly faced. For just when he is able to put it all to the back of his mind, disasters occur. James' embarrassment is all the more acute when just as he seems to be in control his weakness and disability are unexpectedly revealed. For things can still suddenly all go wrong.

One reason for this is an additional hazard which the suction limbs present. Just as they fit easily and snugly round his stumps, so sudden movements can cause the limbs to release their grip. With no other mechanism for holding the legs on, James and his limbs have been known to suddenly part company for no apparent reason! On one occasion James recalls attempting to enter a shop just as a couple were leaving. Trying awkwardly to dodge them was enough to break the suction of the limbs. James collapsed on the pavement in a misshapen heap! It was as if he were falling apart as his feet and legs slipped out of his trousers and he turned to see the horrified faces of both the couple and other passers-by.

James claims that this is an in-built device to keep him humble: just as he begins to think his walking is particularly good, his legs will give way and he will land in this ungainly heap. But sometimes this humiliating experience has had useful side-effects. It was as he was involved in some work for his local church that James found that the 'falling-apart trick' came in very handy. It was the middle of the herring season in Peterhead and the town was full of foreign fishermen. In particular, there was a whole fleet of Russian 'klondykers' moored in the harbour. (Named after the middle men who bought gold from prospectors in the Yukon goldrush, these were boats which bought fish from other boats rather than catching them directly. The nature of the trade meant that the sailors were often in town for some time as the business was transacted.)

It became known that a bookshop in Aberdeen had managed to get access to a large number of Russian Bibles. The Christians in Peterhead could see a great opportunity on their doorsteps. Why not see if any of these fishermen would be willing to accept the Bibles to take back home with them? James eagerly agreed to help.

It was only after the Bibles were delivered to the factory and he sat staring at them on his desk that James began to wonder how on earth he was going to make contact with these men. How could a man with no legs corner Soviet sailors on shore, far less reach them on their ships? He had no idea. He stuffed a couple in his jacket pocket, however, thinking hopefully that he would be prepared should a situation arise.

A few days after the Bibles arrived James was out on a brief errand in the town. He had just popped into the Post Office and he was just making his way back to the car. Unfortunately the weather was wild and he began to regret venturing outside. Rain was splashing into great puddles and it dripped from every gutter. Heading for the car as quickly as he dared, James suddenly noticed them: half a dozen Russian sailors sheltering under the canopy of a shop.

James approached them slowly, completely at a loss as to how to start speaking to the men. How do you walk up to someone you don't know and whose language you can't speak and make them a gift of some Bibles, he thought. He was almost upon them, praying as he went, "Lord, how can I speak to these Russians..?" The answer was unexpected! Suddenly his stick which he had with him slipped on the wet pavement. Loosing his balance, James could feel his legs come apart: they went one way and James went the other. He landed with a splash and a thump on the pavement, just at the Russians' feet!

Gaping in horror at this incredible sight of a man whose legs had just fallen off lying on the ground, the fishermen quickly came to his rescue. They watched in amazement but dawning realisation as James jammed his legs back on and they were able to help him to his feet. In perfect English one of them checked that he was unhurt. He was the ship's surgeon he said but James assured him that he did not require his professional help: only his pride was hurt and his trousers wet and torn. Suddenly realising his chance, however, James fumbled in his pocket for a Bible. Thanking them profusely he asked, "Will you take these from me for your help?" Taking the Bible the Russians were as surprised as they had been by James' sudden descent upon them. "A Bible...in Russian?" they stared. They were flabbergasted. Here they were hundreds of miles from home and some man whose legs had fallen off in front of them in the street had Russian Bibles in his pockets!

Soon they all wanted one and James offered to give them those at the factory. Before long the surgeon and the chief mate were ensconced in James' office looking at the Bibles and drinking coffee. They were delighted with them and explained that although Bibles were not banned by the state any longer, it was extremely difficult to buy them. Knowing this James had been concerned previously that the Russian Bibles may be sold for a large price on the Soviet black market but the genuine interest shown by the men soon set his mind at rest. He was even able to talk to them about his belief in it as God's holy Word and its importance to him.

When the chief mate and his captain returned to see James the next day to ask if he had any more Bibles James was only too delighted to get some.

The Russians also extended an invitation to James to go aboard their freezer-trawler in the bay and have a meal with the captain and the other senior officers. Always keen to try something new he accepted and soon found himself being whisked across the bay in the ship's lifeboat. Arriving at the steep sides of the huge trawler James could see no way for him to get aboard, but the Russians had thought of everything - the lifeboat with James and his companions on board was simply hoisted up by the powerful hauling equipment and James was able to walk on board. With impeccable manners and generous hospitality James was quickly put at ease and they were soon swapping travel stories and experiences of life at sea. They told James of their home port, Leningrad, a beautiful city but one which James had never visited. James got on particularly well with the chief mate, Alexander Karakulov and kept in contact with him long after the klondykers had all gone home.

During that herring season James and his friends had given away more than eight hundred Russian Bibles. They felt that they had somehow contributed to a Buchan 'glasnost' in an effective and far-reaching way. As James recalled the events, however, he was always made to laugh by God's unusual answer to his prayer. God must truly have a sense of humour, he thought, to devise such a dramatic and comical introduction to those Soviet sailors.

James often finds, therefore, that his disability becomes

a means of talking to people rather than a hindrance. In particular, he has often been asked to speak to other disabled people. Prior to his accident James had been ill at ease with disabled people and had always avoided them. It was a shocking revelation to him that he had never considered the disabled as real people before with interests and needs beyond their brave suffering. Suddenly he found that he had much in common with them, especially those who had been injured or bereaved through accidents. He seemed to have the experience and insight to know how to relate to them and be able to empathise. Those whom he spoke to locally and those whom he travelled to meet in Edinburgh and beyond, knew that he spoke from experience and therefore appreciated that he had an understanding of their situation. It was more credible also to witness true faith working in his life, when it was clear that it had been put severely to the test.

Through these contacts James became aware that many disabled people long for some means of regaining or establishing their own identity and want to make use of the capabilities which they have. He also saw that, like most people, this can best be fulfilled by having a job and soon became involved organising this in his own area. He had two disabled men working for him already: Thomas Milne as a salesman and Robert Piric as a machine operator. With only a staff of ten this one in five ratio, not even counting himself, earned the company a 'Fit for Work' award from the Manpower Services Commission. Later this led to him working with the Commission and touring businesses with the Disabled

Resettlement Officer to see if they had the quota of disabled people working for them which is demanded by law.

Whenever he visits businesses in this connection James is able to tell how his own disabled employees contribute to the company. They have certainly not proved to be a handicap. Indeed Thomas knows so many of the local skippers that through this personal contact he has increased ice sales hugely. Robert also fitted in well and is helped by a special chair which the Commission provided when he finds it painful to stand beside his machine all day. When he isn't using it the other boys find it a welcome rest!

It is always a surprise to James when his disability can have such positive effects and he is able to contribute something to the community or to individuals through it. Similarly he is able to work in the church for his Lord, reaching people like the Russians sailors whom he might otherwise not have been able to contact. Even through the press coverage and a subsequent television interview he has made many contacts with people who have enquired particularly about his faith.

"If it begins to explain to people why this has happened to me," he adds, " - that there are things to be done for God or someone who needs to know about him that can only be done or that can only be reached by a man in my situation - then, okay, that's fine and I'm happy to do it. I'm the man for the job. His purposes for our lives are sometimes tough, in fact *without* Christ I don't think that I could make it. But he's taken me through and I'm grateful. That should be enough. If he's taken me through all this so that I can now do something for him, then that's a pretty special bonus and one I'll take hold of - with both hands!"

Although the pain and frustration and inconvenience will perhaps always remain, and memories and nightmares will perhaps never quite be buried, James is confident that the God who has never abandoned him and who holds the future secure will remain with him. It is because of this that he can look ahead with genuine optimism and hope.

"Every day is a challenge," he concludes. "It is a challenge to wake up at 7am, put on my legs and face up to the day ahead. And that day-in, day-out task can make me weary, I suppose. But I can honestly say that I always want to do it. God is, after all, on my side."

MUSSELS AT MIDNIGHT

Stephen Anderson

The story of Stephen Anderson contains enough
excitement and variety for two lifetimes.
From dancing with the Queen to playing polo in the
Egyptian desert; from a farm in Perthshire to the
churches in Scotland. Stephen Anderson has been a
captain in the army, a ski instructor, but above all a
communicator of the gospel.

ISBN 0 906731 93 3

160 pp   pocket paperback

ALICIA

Alicia Simpson

The personal account of Alicia Simpson.

She was born into a Roman Catholic family, became a nun when she was old enough, left the convent, married a nominal Protestant but all the while was being led by God to be ready to trust in Jesus as her Saviour.

This book is suitable for every age-group between thirteen and one hundred.

It is very easy to read.
From Sunday School prize to Old Folks' Home, it will be useful.

ISBN 0 906731 860

64 pp   large paperback

OUT OF THE TIGER'S MOUTH

The Autobiography of
Dr Charles H. Chao

Dramatic escapes from the Chinese authorities were
a feature of Charles Chao's early life.

Not that he was a criminal; just a man determined
to follow his Lord and Master whatever the risks
and sacrifices as he developed the work of
The Reformation Translation Fellowship.

ISBN 1 871676 59 2

160pp   pocket paperback

CHANGING STEP

Jill Beatty

Jill Beatty has never been one to conform.

From her days as a rebellious teenager,
through the ups and downs of army life in the Middle
East during the creation of the modern state of Israel,
followed by a marriage to a backslidden Christian
which ultimately led to a turbulent and often difficult
life as a pastor's wife, she has come to a strong faith in
God's leading and providing.

ISBN 1 871676 68 1

160pp   pocket paperback

HE FOUND ME

Ten Christians tell how they first came to know the Lord
Jesus and what he has done for them since then.
They include

Sarah Chan
brought up as a Buddhist in Hong Kong who
now works among the Jews of London.

Donald Macleod
a professor of theology in Edinburgh.

Lady Rose
born in a castle.

Jeanette Fyfe
A former Jehovah's Witness.

J. Douglas Macmillan
Pastor and writer.

Margo Macaskill
Pastor's wife.